Praise for *Sacred Wild*

"Welles offers insights, exercises, meditations, and rituals informed by her practice and inspired by divine moments. ... Timely and necessary, this book is a call to action to serve and protect the land."

—**IRISANYA MOON**, author of various Pagan Portals books

"Welles weaves together her land-based practices with great skill and care. ... As readers, we're brought into these animistic traditions not as mere observers but active participants."

—**BRANDON WESTON**, author of *Ozark Folk Magic*

"*Sacred Wild* is exactly what the modern spiritual person needs. It's a gentle but firm reminder of our sacred connection the natural wild that exists within and outside of us."

—**COURTNEY WEBER**, author of *Hekate* and *Sacred Tears*

"Elyse's authenticity and commitment to the land spirits is evident: she lives the practice that she preaches."

—**JAMIE DELLA**, author of *A Box of Magick*

"A cozy, warm, and intimate call to connecting to the spaces around us.... Welles takes us on a guided tour around our everyday environments, offering anecdotes, points of consideration, and approaches we can employ to connect."

—**BENJAMIN STIMPSON**, author of *Ancestral Whispers*

"No witch's reference library is complete without *Sacred Wild*! It's a grounded and fascinating guide."

—**HEATHER WILDFLOWER**, social media influencer (@heather.wildflower)

"We are guided to not only remember [our connection to the land] but to develop and nourish it. Through exercises that are as simple as they are profound, the reader is empowered to explore the depths of this connection."

—**COBY MICHAEL**, author of *Poison Path Herbal*

"*Sacred Wild* guides readers through precise crafting, detailing how we can all be reborn ordained apprentices of sacred lands."
—**MAWIYAH KAI EL-JAMAH BOMANI**, author of *Conjuring the Calabash*

"From India to Switzerland to the Pennsylvania of her childhood, Welles walks lightly and respectfully through the world, ever attuned to the eternal powers of place."
—**LINDA RAEDISCH**, author of *The Old Magic of Christmas*

"A treasure trove for anyone looking to connect with the land spirits. With her clear and concise writing style, Elyse offers unique exercises."
—**S. CONNOLLY**, author of *Wortcunning for Daemonolatry*

"Evocative and poetic, while at the same time exceedingly grounded and practical."
—**DEBORAH BLAKE**, author of *The Eclectic Witch's Book of Shadows*

"A beautiful, thorough guide to exploring the magic inherent in our landscape. Rooted in building relationships and reciprocity, Elyse guides the reader through insightful prompts and meaningful exercises."
—**JAMIE WAGGONER**, author of *Hades*

"Welles weaves ancient animistic principles with modern reflective practices, making each chapter a stepping stone toward a deeper sense of place in the natural world."
—**MANNY MORENO**, managing editor at *The Wild Hunt*

"Welles draws on history, folklore, mythology, and her own personal practice to offer a plethora of ideas and inspiration to those seeking a stronger bond with the spirits, stories, and soul of the land."
—**STEELE ALEXANDRA DOURIS**, author of *Spirits, Seers & Séances*

"Welles is an affable guide for both neophyte and experienced Pagans as she treks through the brambles."
—**RICK DE YAMPERT**, author of *Crows and Ravens*

"The perfect book to help you connect to the wildness of the world."
—**EMMA KATHRYN**, author of *Season Songs* and *Witch Life*

SACRED *Wild*

About the Author

Elyse Welles holds a master's degree in spiritual studies and is a high priestess in the eclectic Faery Tradition with a practice centered on land spirits and sacred places (numina). She cohosts *The Magick Kitchen Podcast*, leads pagan pilgrimages to the temples of Greece, and teaches nature-based spirituality online. Elyse lives between the ancient temple of Artemis in Greece and Havre de Grace, Maryland. Visit her at SeekingNumina.com.

AN INVITATION TO CONNECT WITH
SPIRITS of the LAND

ELYSE WELLES
Foreword by Amy Blackthorn

First Edition
First Printing, 2025

Cover design by Shannon McKuhen
Interior art by the Llewellyn Art Department

Library of Congress Cataloging-in-Publication Data (Pending)
ISBN: 978-0-7387-7976-8

Llewellyn Publications
A Division of Llewellyn Worldwide Ltd.
2143 Wooddale Drive
Woodbury, MN 55125-2989
www.llewellyn.com

Printed in the United States of America

FSC www.fsc.org MIX Paper | Supporting responsible forestry FSC® C005010

GPSR Representation:
UPI-2M PLUS d.o.o., Medulićeva 20, 10000 Zagreb, Croatia
matt.parsons@upi2mbooks.hr

Also by Elyse Welles

What the Water Remembers

Contents

Exercises

Foreword

My father was in the navy before I was born, so the habit of moving every two years was ingrained in our family. To this day, every two years or so, I start looking at the packing boxes my books come in and say, "Man, that's a good box. I better keep it. Just in case." I've never had a friend I knew since birth.

But knowing Elyse is instant friendship. Whether you met her thirty seconds ago or ten years ago, she is a true friend, a trusted priestess, and a caring soul. You feel like you have known her all your life. Elyse has lived all over, and as a fellow "new kid," I can tell you figuring out how to connect with the newest place is sometimes harder than connecting to an entire new friend group with each new experience.

Elyse has worked her entire life to get to this point, the precipice of your awareness, ready to dive into the role of author with the grace and power of cliff diver, ready to spear into the waters of your emotion to connect you to the lands you only think you know. The land is quiet with new faces, but Elyse helps you understand where you have been and how that leads you to the land spirits you reside with now.

In the spring of 2020, the global lockdown to try to stem the tide of COVID-19 led people to exploring their homes, yards, neighborhoods, and more. "The land is healing" and "Nature is returning" were common rallying cries. We wanted to see that our sequestering was worth it and produced a visual cue. It's hard to experience numbers on a page. The truth is most of what people were seeing wasn't just the land attempting to connect with us; it was people taking time to look at the land on which they live and *see it*, likely for the first time. Sometimes all we need is a change in perspective to understand where someone is coming from. Even if that someone is the land spirits or the city surrounding you.

Whether you rent, own, or experience the nomad life, the land you are standing on is sacred, just as you are. We tend to travel as humans, to seek out new experiences and delight in new sights. It's the same reason that vacation sunsets never seem to match the sunset at home. And it's also the reason most traffic accidents happen within a few miles of one's home. Once we are in a familiar space, we can drop our guard, because we like to think that the familiar is safe. In this book, Elyse's soft, conversational style really helps us understand that our land spirits are helping spirits seeking a relationship with us, with the people who have come before, and with the people who will come after. It's like introducing yourself to new neighbors when they move in. They might be standoffish with new people, or you may have just made a friend for life. Elyse's work helps us create connections so that we can embrace the space in which we are, right now.

Her guidance on plant allies was of course the chapter I was looking forward to most of all. The exercise on working with mushrooms was a true joy because I live hear the mushroom capital of the world, Kennett Square, Pennsylvania. With such a rich history of nature bonding with humans, Kennett Square offers a unique perspective on developing relationships with the fungi nation.

By entering into sacred relationship with the areas around you, you needn't travel the globe to find magic. You can find it in your own backyard. The travel is just a bonus.

—Amy Blackthorn, author of the Blackthorn's Botanicals series

INTRODUCTION

Heeding the Call of the Sacred Wild

The call of the sacred wild often begins with a seemingly simple draw to the outdoors. There are some signs that your land spirits have been reaching out to you already. If you're a gardener, you've met the spirits of the plants, intentionally or not, and enjoying gardening harmoniously with the plants around you is a great first step in working with land spirits more intentionally. Have you ever found yourself noticing the winds shifting and feeling the call of a storm before it hits? This is the sacred wild communicating with you, sending you a kind warning so you can prepare.

If you know your day goes better when you've had a chance to sit outside with your coffee in the morning and you're making the choice to do that, you've begun heeding the call. If animals feel at ease around you and you're able to pick up on their needs, whether they're pets or outdoor critters, that's a sign that the spirits of nature are feeling connected to you for what you've been doing, perhaps unconsciously. If these things haven't happened for you, they will when you begin implementing the workings of this book.

The idea for this book came from the land spirits themselves. I felt its impending arrival as I stood in the fullness of the moon, watching her rise as the sun slowly set. Out of nowhere, a fox stepped into my view, and we made direct eye contact and didn't move for many minutes. I felt it as clearly as if the fox had spoken to me: I was to prepare to receive a message.

That night, I stepped out onto the balcony, ready to receive. Hair still wet from the shower, I ran my comb through my hair and offered the fallen strands to the land spirits. The purest gift, hair is the essence of our soul in many cultures, my native Greece included. I let it fly on the wind and followed its flight to the line of *pevka*, the ancient Greek pine trees older than Greece herself, protected still for the home it lends the Athena owls. And as my eyes rose to where the full moon peeked through the branches, the idea for this book arrived.

This is the magic of the land spirits. They are subtle, quiet, and calm—but wildly present. And if we can learn to listen to them, and answer their requests, we can build a trust that will transform our definitions of what spirit relationships can be. They are the key to having right relationship with the land, and right relationship with the land is the key to a grounded, fulfilled, and present life.

My own experiences with land spirits began intuitively when I was a child growing up in rural Pennsylvania. We were fortunate to have a pond, woods, a small orchard of fruit trees, and a lovely field to play in. I would mix "potions" with leaves, sticks, and acorns, asking the plants who wants to be included. I'd ask the birds to help me with my math homework, counting them as I watched flocks fly overhead. And when I had a bad day at school, I'd retreat to the woods, crying against my favorite trees.

As an adult, I pursued formal witchcraft training, completing my initiation as a high priestess of the eclectic Faery Tradition, a tradition that focuses on animism and nature's cycles. I began to make connections about the practices I was taught by the land as a child. Over a decade later, I have since traveled to dozens of countries to seek *numina*, sacred places. In fact, Seeking Numina is the umbrella under which I teach the Path of the Sacred Wild and host retreats at Greece's numina. I have lived and traveled all over the world and in very different spiritual ecosystems, encountering land spirits from the desert of Bahrain in the Arabian Gulf, the forests of the East Coast of the US, the incomparable papyrus banks of the Nile in Egypt (another nationality I hold), and now Greece, where my father is from. I completed a master's degree with specialization in the syncretism of earth-based folk practices around the world. And in my sacred poetry, articles, and journalistic writing for magazines and anthology collections, I have further explored the power of land spirits. For almost fifteen years, the land has been guiding me. And this book is the culmination of this guidance.

Who This Book Is For

This is a book for people who are ready to connect to the sacred wild by meeting the land spirits, whom I have found to be both the gatekeepers and teachers of the deeper connections to nature. Working with land spirits and following the path of the sacred wild is for everyone, regardless of your spiritual or religious beliefs. Witches, pagans, Druids, Heathens, healers, and those who prefer no labels at all will benefit from the addition of land spirits work because it anchors us in the land we live on and the lands we travel to. If you are called to the language of trees, the friendship of wildlife, and the stewardship of land, this is the path for you.

The sacred wild is an all-encompassing term that I use for the wisdom, magic, and growth we find in the cycles of the Wheel of the Year and the moon. We feel the sacred wild within ourselves when we are moved by the beauty of nature. It is the healing and clarity that comes with embracing wildness: when we swim in the sea, flip a rock to watch the bugs, chat with and feed the local birds, or roll down a hill.

Who Are the Land Spirits?

Land spirits are the guardians of that sacred space. To be clear, these spirits have never been human; they are eternal beings, rather than immortal, because they cannot be destroyed. Not even wildfires or extreme weather can hurt them, although the suffering of the creatures and plants in their dominion certainly angers and saddens them, to use human words for the way affected lands change after devastation.

Land spirits have many names, but they are common to every culture on Earth. They are in turns both feared and revered, but when treated with respect and honor, they can be our greatest ally.

They are not metaphors. They are the primordial beings that reside with—and in a sense, preside over—the land they're on.

Land spirits deepen your roots. Evoke your highest self. Ground you in the land you call home, and as guardians of the land, aid strongly in protection magic. They can teach you how to experience and absorb the energy of sacred places and to take the lessons of their energy home with you.

Land spirits are both simple and complex. They're ever-present but require special tuning to find their frequency. Building relationships is within everyone's ability but also requires time and energy. When invited, land spirits will always bring you into magical moments of presence and empowerment in nature.

Relationships with land spirits allow us to remember how we are connected to everything on Earth, from the worms to the clouds. Land spirits also remind us of the fleeting nature of this life, for better or worse. They ask us to be present and live in the moment, while recognizing that all the burdens and overwhelm we might experience are small in the grand scheme of nature's power.

Land spirits bring only respite and grounding. And with this peace comes happiness and fulfillment.

How to Use This Book

In this book, you'll learn how to recognize and understand what land spirits are and how to build relationships with them. The exercises and chapters will encourage you to go beyond vague perceptions of the elements and instead build relationships with the real spirits of nature. I recommend completing the chapters in order, as each chapter builds on the previous one. But these rituals and exercises are designed to be revisited again and again, to encounter new land spirits and rekindle relationships with old ones.

Before beginning the exercises of this book, consider choosing a land spirits journal. This will include your workings and notes from this book, but it can also grow beyond that as you explore and expand your relationships with land spirits. You can bring it on vacations and trips to new places to record your experiences with the land spirits there too. You also may want to join my Facebook group, Seekers of the Sacred Wild, where I share additional resources, answer questions, and build community with readers like you.

Many of the exercises are reflective journal prompts. If you hate writing, reflect in different ways: a video blog that's only for you to see; audio recordings, again for yourself only; or a painting or abstract art exploration, such as a collage. Mind mapping can work too: visual displays of single words in their relationship to each other. A quick internet search will find examples for you. When you reflect on your feelings of each prompt, instead of writing full sentences, consider writing words that come to mind in different sizes or fonts or drawing lines or circles around them.

The point of these exercises is for you to reflect alone. If you want to talk these through with mentors or trusted friends or chosen family, that's fine. Some wonderful insights about ourselves come from open conversations like that. But your deepest reflections should stay private so you don't color your writing or creating with that other person in mind. This is a process of *self*-reflection, by and for your*self.*

Humans need to listen now more than ever to the lessons of the land, as we live lives so removed from the cycles of nature. We're only a few generations removed from a world dependent on right relationship with the land, and it's time to return to that path. If you picked up this book, chances are the land is calling you home. Will you heed their call?

CHAPTER 1

Spirits of Place

The term *spirit of place* covers all spirits you may find in a particular location. In Oman, the djinn fly. Leprechauns, brownies, sprites, and other fae folk grace the forests and hills of Ireland. If you travel north to Norway and Denmark, you'll find the *landvaettir*, alive and well. The Romans called upon and honored the *genius loci*: the spirit of place. And living here in Greece, I have met and honored the *stoixeia*, the Greek word for "land spirits," in the wilds of Arcadia and throughout Greece. There are many types of spirits of place that go by many names. However, they are not all specifically land spirits, which are the presiding spirit of place in any given area.

In this chapter, I'll discuss the many different spirits of place you'll encounter on your quest to meet land spirits. Spirits of place are important to recognize because they are more active than the land spirits themselves—they seem to notice humans and historically have a relationship with them. The stories of faeries from cultures around the world support this awareness, and it can extend into a fear or discomfort with experiencing spirits of place. Many stories of the fae are fraught with warnings: "Never say thank you to the faeries," "Never give them gifts because they'll always expect more," "Don't step inside a faerie circle," and more warnings were given to me when I was a child growing up reading fairy tales. I heard them again on tours through Ireland. And I see these themes crop up on social media too, even by other practitioners of land connection. But in my experience with land spirits work, the spirits of place like faeries and nymphs are simply protective of their land. Like most spirits, humans included, they only have a negative expression when they feel they need to protect their home. I encourage you to have an open mind about spirits of place and the relationships you can build with them, as they are important to the land spirits and therefore important to anyone seeking to work deeply with the land.

In this chapter, you'll learn how to recognize the different spirits of place, and in the exercises, you'll learn how to work with them to get their seal of approval so that you can reach deeper and connect with the land spirits themselves.

Animism

The core of working with spirits of place, including land spirits, animism is the belief that all creatures great and small, plants, inanimate objects, and natural phenomena like thunderstorms, hurricanes, tornadoes, and wildfires have a living spirit or soul to them. Some animists draw the line at creatures, from fish to mammals to birds; others include plants but not weather or inanimate objects. Still others have their own limits, where they might include human-made items—from magical tools to plastic cups or cars.

Witches, pagans, and spiritual practitioners tend to believe that animals (including fish, insects, etc.), people, crystals, and plants have a living spirit. Your practice might view these spirits in different ways, but to feel they are enspirited is a belief common in most spiritual practices. When we extend that understanding further to include not just the trees in the forest but the grove they grow in; when we include the snowstorm itself when we discuss the spirits of the land in midwinter; when we embrace not just crystals but sand from the beach or rocks found on a hike as innately alive, communicative, and otherwise spirited—that is animism.

In an animist worldview, it is easy to accept that the land itself can have a soul of its own. Embracing this even further, we can accept that that being has inhabited the land and will continue to *ad infinitum*—they have seen and felt all that the land has and will continue to see and feel all that the land does. And then it becomes clear that it is they who keep watch over the trees and creatures—and us, if we reach out.

Animism is also the acknowledgment that spirits have free will and autonomy. When we engage in land spirits magic, we are calling on these spirits to choose to connect, an expression of animistic belief in spiritual autonomy.

There are hard animists that find spirits in human-made items, from computers to cars, and there are natural animists that simply see the spirit in living things, from insects to animals and even to bacteria. Personally, I find myself somewhere in between. As enspirited beings ourselves, we can create things with spirits, such as poppets or talismans, but I don't find everything, particularly plastic or utilitarian items like a plunger or dish soap, to have a spirit to it. But I do bless and thank my technology and appliances when I cleanse my home, asking them to continue working in good order and thanking them for their service in my home. I also find my car, phone, and computer to have a spirit to them, as they are tools that I create sacred magic with by documenting and traveling to sacred places with them. And my shoes that touch ground in sacred sites receive a funerary farewell when it's time for them to be retired.

Exercise: REFLECTIONS ON ANIMISM

Choose a favorite tree or natural spot and bring your land spirits journal. Take a few minutes to look around you and reflect on your own beliefs about animism. Remember that your understanding of the spiritual will constantly shift and grow; journaling and reflecting on your beliefs should not merely reinforce them. Reflection is an opportunity to let the ego be heard, and then you can begin to question your beliefs and adjust them as you feel based on your increasing experiences.

Your attribution of animism will likely shift as you grow on this path. I didn't set out with an animistic view of shoes or cars, but here we are. The lessons of animism are expansive and humbling. Animism is a key principle in land spirits work because you are looking for the spirit of land itself, and through this work, you will also encounter fae, plant spirits, weather spirits, and more. It's important to have an open mind to the way these spirits will feel, and getting attuned to the frequencies of each over time will hone your discernment.

Elementals

If this isn't your first book on paganism, witchcraft, or spirit work, you've likely come across elementals. Elementals are closely connected to land spirits, but they are not the same. In brief, the elementals are denizens of the four, sometimes five, elements that make up our world: earth, air, fire, water, and, in some traditions, spirit. All elementals are spiritual beings associated with a particular element, such as jinn/djinn being elementals of fire, or sylphs being the elementals of air. In some witchcraft traditions, there are specific beings called upon in each quarter that are referred to as the elementals, the guardians, the watchtowers, or other secret names. And in Druidry, they are called upon in triplicate as land, sea, and sky.

Elementals are distinct from land spirits, although you'll encounter elementals out in nature. Elementals are mobile. They are the spirit of the element itself. Wind spirits, as an expression of the air elementals, travel many miles. Sea waves and hurricanes, and the sea spirits found within them, are expressions of water elementals, and they, too, by nature, travel. In short, the elementals are expressions of the element. Land spirits are not connected to any specific element, and they are tied to a specific place, and all elements are present on their land. Calling on the elementals with the land spirits to support you is a powerful practice, and when you work with land spirits, the elementals are strongly felt: the wind picks up, rain clouds shift overhead, the sun shines warmly, and the trees can feel like they're dancing in connection with you. Having an understanding of the elementals you are noticing when you work with the land is a powerful context for the spirits you might feel.

Elementals are called upon with intention in many spiritual traditions. Popular elementals called upon in alchemical, witchcraft, and pagan traditions are as follows:

- Sylphs for air
- Undines for water

- Salamanders for fire
- Gnomes for earth

Names for elemental spirits originated in works by the alchemist Paracelsus, a sixteenth-century physician, alchemist, lay theologian, and philosopher from Germany. In his book *A Book on Nymphs, Sylphs, Pygmies, and Salamanders, and on the Other Spirits*, published posthumously in 1566, he writes of his scientific observation of land spirits and discusses the importance of including elementals in the Christian worldview. He asserts that they aren't demonic or competitive with the Christian God but instead need to be revered as part of the creation story.[1] While his intentions were pure in his reverence for nature spirits, for modern witches to call on the elementals with these names without the understanding of where they come from has always struck me as odd. And if you've been calling them in and not really feeling much in return, you're not alone!

The names Paracelsus chose for the elementals he observed are somewhat arbitrary. Salamanders at the time were thought to protect from fire damage, which is why he named the fire elementals as such, and he uses the word *sylphs* for air elementals and *undines* for water elementals, which are their first appearance in literature with no solid grounding in their origins or meanings.

I'll be honest: I have never felt a gnome in my entire life when calling these guys into circle with my coven or in private ceremony. In my experience, these beings are too vague and undefined, and in my own rituals, I call in the cultural terminology that aligns better for me with the way I've actually encountered the elementals. Here in Greece, I call on the nymphs of each element: the Anemoi (the Four Winds) or the aurae, the nymphs of wind; the Hesperides, nymphs of sunset; the naiads of the river and the nereids and oceanids of the sea; and the dryads and oreads of the trees and mountains.

---

1. Paracelsus, *Four Treatises of Theophrastus von Hohenheim, Called Paracelsus*, vol. 1, ed. C. Lilian Temkin, George Rosen, Gregory Zilboorg, and Henry E. Sigerist (Johns Hopkins Press, 1941), 223–25.

That doesn't mean gnomes don't exist; they just have never been present anywhere I've called on them, and they may not be present where you live. For example, the jinn are fire spirits found in Oman. If you're calling on them in Wisconsin, you might not get an answer. But when I called on them when I lived in Bahrain, an island near Oman in the Arabian Gulf, I felt their presence. When I call them here in Greece, they are fainter. Try out different terms and see which feels right. You might, instead, feel most comfortable calling them in without names, and there's nothing wrong with that. With prolonged experience, they may even tell you a name, which we will talk about in chapter 2.

Consider how you want to approach elementals. There is an older approach to magic that encourages practitioners to command gods and spirits.[2] This is not the way I recommend beginning any relationships with spirits, and especially not elementals or land spirits, as it plays into patriarchal views of dominance rather than reciprocal relationship. Another common way to invoke the elements to join in a ritual is to use the Wiccan phrase: to "summon, stir, and call [them] forth." I learned this invocation in my own initiation process with the eclectic Faery Tradition. This phrasing may not resonate with you, as it tends not to resonate with me, because the elements are inherent around us: we don't have to summon them as much as invite them or honor their existing presence.

When wildfires threaten my home in Greece, as happens every summer, unfortunately, I call on the air elementals to calm the high winds that spread the flames and ask them instead to help put out the spreading fires. I call on the fire elementals to end the suffering of creatures and plants of Earth too, essentially inviting them to recognize the suffering they're causing. Commanding or summoning the fire spirits to halt or rain spirits to fall dangerously out of season (summer rains are a danger, causing mudslides) is about control. But the magic I'm doing is about balance, and inviting the elements to come to that understanding is my purpose. The language I use is "Guardians of the East, Element of Air, Aurae of the Four

---

2. Aleister Crowley, *The Book of the Goetia of Solomon the King* (Society for the Propagation of Religious Truth, 1904), vii.

Anemoi, I invite you to join me in this rite to end the fires in Greece," or something similar to state the purpose of the given ritual.

Exercise: FINDING YOUR CORE ELEMENT

Commune with the elementals on your land. Next time there is a storm, go outside and meditate, dance, feel the rain on your skin. Feel the winds on a windy day. Communing with earth is a constant in a way, if you spend time with trees, herbs, flowers, or other growing things. But if you have an earthquake or plant new plants or trees, this is a good time to check in with earth as an elemental. Have a bonfire outdoors and see how the land responds—if you live near wildfires, check in with the land spirits (from far away from the actual fires for your own safety) and feel the energetic shifts that the fires are causing. How does the land feel now compared to when there were no fires? Record your experiences.

When you communed with each, did one stick out to you? Research the elementals and how they appear in your chart to see if this lines up. If it doesn't, is there a part of yourself you're repressing? Land spirits are great allies in unlocking our core potentials and true selves, as we'll discuss in later chapters.

Other Spirits of Place

While land spirits are the dominant spirit of a place, they facilitate and "reign" over a specific area inhabited by many spirits. There are land spirits of varying size and influence found everywhere in the world, but they are never the only spirit of place. In some places like Greece, deities can be one of the spirits of place you'll find in a given location: for example, in the valley of Artemis I live in in Greece. Other spirits of place might reside in a particular dell, a grove, or even a single tree within a larger forest: the groves of olives within the valley also have the spirit of Olive. There are also the spirits of the animals that live there and the people who have lived there or currently live there.

There is no hierarchy of spirits in a patriarchal sense. Competition and possession are human constructs. But there are spirits that are stronger presences than others. The land spirits are the oldest, strongest presence of the land that does hold a sort of dominion over mortal creatures. These are the categories and terms I use for the different types of spirits of place you might encounter beyond the land spirits themselves. It takes practice and time to connect with land spirits, and in the meantime, you may encounter some spirits of place more easily than others. Enjoy this journey and use your land spirits journal to document your questions and observations.

Exercise: NOTICING YOUR LAND

When you go outside, for any reason—yard work, to head for your car, to get the mail—do you feel an energetic shift? What does it feel like? Tune in to it on your walks outdoors, no matter how brief, and record your experiences.

Animal Spirits of Place

Emissaries of the Land

Creatures of the land like mammals, insects, and birds may act as emissaries for the land spirits. This is my preferred term, because they serve as a sort of front line to the land spirits' energy. The critters of the forest give us so many clues about the land spirits' energy. They are what we notice and see first, and if the animals are welcoming you, the land often is too.

Another way to look at them is as familiars for the land, or even fetches (parts of a spirit sent off separate from the whole). When a land spirit needs to send us a message or connect with us, they often take the form or enlist the help of animals, such as birds, snakes, or even insects. Like the fox in the story that opens this book, they often relay messages. When you are most in need of comfort or protection, don't be surprised if an animal you're not used to seeing finds its way to you. If you ask for a sign from the land that they've accepted your offering or request for aid, listen for birdsong or look for animals to appear. Land spirits often communicate through emissaries like squirrels, foxes, crow, deer, or other creatures. Butterflies, ladybugs, praying mantises, crickets, and other insects are also common emissaries.

While deities and spirit guides can also use animals as messengers, the message of the land spirits will be clear. In my experience, land spirits prefer to send wild animals rarely seen, such as owls, foxes, bears, fawns, or even toads. If you see an animal that you know prefers to avoid humans, but it chooses not to run from or avoid you, then you can safely accept that as a message from a land spirit. Likewise, if an insect or a bird does something strange or unusual, like land on your arm or sit on the table in front of you, this is a sign that the land is approving of your efforts of connection.

When you begin leaving offerings and communing with your land, pay extra attention for signs of a message from the land spirits. They might be in need, or there might be a change coming for you or your land that you can't yet perceive. If there's inclement weather the land needs your help to prepare for or you have had unwanted or unexpected visitors coming, don't be surprised if the land spirits give you a heads up. If an animal is behaving oddly, then it's usually a signal for us to pay attention. However, I do offer this one practical warning. Wild animals acting oddly can also be a sign of rabies or other illness as well. Do not approach a wild animal for any reason, even if it is clearly an omen.

When we get signs from animals, the immediate temptation is to race to look up what it means online. But meanings are personal. There is overlap, of course, and that's where the accepted definitions of signs come from. Shared personal gnosis leads to a sort of verification that can be more comfortable than trusting our intuition, but if you're on this path of spiritual growth, trusting your intuition is a part of it.

Notice your initial reaction to the animal; remember what you were thinking of when it showed up or earlier that day. If your grandfather loved cardinals, as my great-grandfather did, and one lands on the deck chair next to you while you're talking about him, as has happened for my mother and me, the meaning is simple: my grandfather is with us for that moment, sending his love. I can look it up and learn that cardinals mean good luck, but I know the meaning is personal to our family as well.

The meanings of the animal messengers we see are deeper than one word or single phrase of guidance, and they are often the start of more signs to come. Animal messengers come in times of transition and are the most relatable way land spirits can reach us.

Vassals of the Land

Specific types of animals, often in community with each other, serve as what I call vassals of the land. These emissaries of the land have a special presence more noticeable compared to other creatures you might encounter there. These are the animals that dominate the location and are charged with its protection because of their loyalty to it. They're the first animals you'll see and the last to see you off when you leave. Or they might not be visible, but their energy is palpable. These animals could be foxes, specific bird species, squirrels, or even something rarely seen, like bears or wild boars. In Susquehanna State Park, there are vultures that nest and fly around me each time I visit. In Aegina, a small island in the Aegean off the coast of mainland Greece, it is the fallow deer that serve as vassals—interestingly, I've never seen them anywhere else in Greece. The role of vassals is to be a living presence on the land and keep it safe; they'll report back to the land spirits with any big actions that need to be taken. Again, there's no patriarchal hierarchy: these animals aren't subservient to the land spirits. But as living creatures who experience birth and death, they occupy a different role from the timeless beings that are the genii loci or *stoixeia*, but both work toward the same goal of safety.

If the animals see something amiss and they choose to get the land spirits involved, everyone will know. I've observed this firsthand in Greece. Due to high heat and sun levels, wildfires are a dangerous reality here from late June to late August each year—a season that grows in length and intensity yearly. Most wildfires in Greece are started by arson, sadly. The gulls of the sea watch the waters and shorelines here, quite vigilantly. You'll hear their calls of discontent, and the land and the weather spirits will respond in kind. If kids start a fire they shouldn't on a beach in wildfire season, a high wind will come and blow it out. If they persist, they might find the waves wash up higher than they should and overtake their campsite. Of course, humans do get involved too, putting out fires and educating in schools against these activities. But it is the land that acts first to protect itself.

Exercise: FINDING THE EMISSARIES AND VASSALS OF YOUR LAND

In your land spirits journal, begin a list of animals, birds, and insects you see, how many, and the date. Do any give you a feeling of acknowledgment? Documenting the mundane helps us see the spiritual hidden in plain sight. As your list of sightings grows, you'll hopefully notice any anomalies, as well as the patterns of animals. Can you identify the emissaries? Are any of these acting as vassals?

Other Spirits You Might Encounter on the Land

Beyond the creatures and spirits of place, in any given place, you will also encounter the energies of other beings that exist in that space, such as plants and people.

Plant Spirits

Plant spirits are the spirits of a particular plant, as well as an expression of the spirit of that species of plant. For example, a particular gardenia bush may have a specific energy that you connect with, but it also carries the spirit of Gardenia, imbuing those who stop and smell its flowers with its gifts of clarity and refinement.[3] Plant spirits are the focus of chapter 6.

Spirits of People

The spirits of people can include the spirits of the people who live there now and the spirits of the people who have died on that land. These spirits may be present and conscious, as some ghosts are. In my experience, they tend to be the residual feelings and impressions of the feelings and emotions presiding over the times these people are living in. If this is a place with no people, like a state park or a hunting ground, consider the emotions brought there when people do visit. They linger there too.

An extension of the individual human spirits is the residual emotions of impactful events. Battlefields, cemeteries, cities, sites of large or frequent

3. John Henry Ingram, *Flora Symbolica; or, the Language and Sentiment of Flowers* (London: Frederick Warne and Co., 1870), 357.

protests, and other places where people congregate in situations with high emotions (positive or negative) will hold a layer of human spiritual activity. This is best understood to be an egregore.

The Egregore

All these spirits of a place, including land spirits themselves, all coalesce to create an egregore that is distinct and changing. *Egregore* is an occult concept derived from the ancient Greek word ἐγρήγορος, *egrēgoros*, meaning "wakeful."[4] You can think of an egregore like the zeitgeist, but instead of being the overarching spirit of the times we live in, it is the feeling of the place in which you are.

When somebody says they don't like "the vibe" of Chicago or love "the energy" of Portland, Oregon, they're talking about the egregore without realizing it. Notice the examples are usually cities: anywhere with a higher concentration of humans to nature, you'll feel the egregore first and have to work harder to find the land spirits.

It's important to remember that even if your intention is to only connect with land spirits, animals, or other nonhuman entities, the human effect on the energy of a place is significant. It's likely that the egregore is the first energy you'll encounter, and the human influence—by humans of the present and the past—is the loudest part of the egregore. Take note of the energies you feel and be prepared to acknowledge that the first layer to meet you will be this egregore. We'll work more with connecting to egregores and urban land spirits in chapter 7.

Meditation: MEETING THE SPIRITS OF PLACE

This is a meditation you can do with your land to engage all your senses. The only requirement for this meditation is to be outside. You may also choose to bring a cup of tea or a glass of water to pour out on the ground in offering before meditating.

---

4. Mark Stavish, *Egregores: The Occult Entities That Watch Over Human Destiny* (Inner Traditions, 2018), 15.

This meditation is best repeated often, at least once during each season, to get a holistic feel for your land. Consider recording yourself reading it. Bring your journal or an audio recorder to record these observations when you're finished.

Close your eyes and breathe deeply. What does the air smell like? Name each scent you can. How does the air feel as it enters your lungs? Picture that air as a bright light. Maybe it's golden, maybe it's a warm green color—whichever resonates with nature's healing power the most for you. As it enters your body, feel it spread out and nourish your soul. Allow yourself to feel the air cleansing you, blessing you, with its warm, bright light. Remind yourself that nature is your home too.

How does it feel to be here? The wind on your skin, on your face, through your hair, rustling your clothes: What does that feel like? What is the temperature? Do you have goosebumps? Is it humid or dry?

Now, listen. What do you hear? How many distinct bird calls? Can you hear insects? How high and leafy are the trees? Do you hear the sounds of humans—cars, sirens, airplanes? Running water? Squirrels, dogs barking? Waves crashing?

Next, tune in to your sixth sense. What is the energy of this place? How does it feel to be here? If memories come up, feel them. How do they make you feel?

Open your eyes. What do you see? Really look past the things you don't usually notice anymore: the wind chime hanging from the porch, the pile of pallets you're someday going to use for a raised garden bed—look at all of it. Where is it being claimed by nature? Where can you clean and prepare this space to be more comfortable for the spirits of your land? Feel the connection you have with the land. Notice your body as a part of this landscape. Remember: when the land spirits are calm, you will be calmer. Feel the warm light of air in your body with each inhale, and remember: we are all connected.

Write or record your observations and your questions. See if you can start identifying the birds you're noticing, the animals, the bugs, the trees and plants around you. And repeat as needed to drop into connection with the land spirits.

CHAPTER 2
Land Spirits Around You

Land spirits are not metaphors or archetypes of energy. They are literal, existing spirits. They are the chief among all spirits of place, which together create a team of balanced beings with different roles and personalities. In this chapter, we will explore the elders: the natural places in which you will find land spirits, and the ways you can connect with their energy in your spiritual practice.

Everyone's land has a spirit. The land spirits of your home won't limit themselves to the boundaries of human-assigned property lines, however. Your neighbors, unless your home consists of dozens of acres, would likely be connecting with the same land spirit, if they chose to reach out. But as you build relationships with them, they might favor your part of their land more than others.

The size of their domain is different for every spirit. In a forest as massive as the Black Forest in Germany, Brocéliande in France, or George Washington and Jefferson National Forests in Virginia, for example, there are many land spirits within their bounds. Those forests' names are human-given, and their boundaries are human-made, so again, the land spirits will have their own boundaries. Particular valleys within the forest will have a different land spirit than a rocky point 200 acres away, even though they're both considered by humans to be inhabiting the same forest. Forests are ecosystems, natural communities for plants, animals, insects, and bacteria. So too are they communities of spirits. Individual trees, caves, or rock formations might have their own spirit too.

The Land Spirit

Land spirits are eternal beings with deep, abiding understandings of the natural world: the blip of human change isn't on their radar. The biggest truth about land spirits is that they are the spirits in this world that are the least tied to human interests. They are not here to give advice on human matters. While they can, and should, be a reliable part of your spirit team for many reasons this book explores, they won't give you direct input on if you should take that new job or not, or what to do about the way your date went last night. Land spirits do not weigh in on—or, frankly, care about—the details of our human lives. They aren't invested in human progress like deities or spirit guides are. But that doesn't mean they won't help you.

They don't need the ins and outs of what you're going through to protect you or bring you comfort. Once our human egos can move past the initial inclination of feeling offended by the indifference of land spirits, it's actually quite comforting to lean on them in times of strife. Like many animal companions you might already have in your life, they don't need to know what a 401(k) is to help you relax and stop stressing about retirement. Land spirits are rooting for you, pun fully intended.

The Elders of the Land

In any natural space, there are elders, the extremely old formations and other natural elements. These locations are where land spirits are most acutely felt. They are the elders of the land because they are the most foundational things of a given place. These can be deserts, boulders, rivers, lakes, and mountains, and in smaller locations like your own neighborhood, they are the oldest trees or unmoved rocks of the area. Standing stones are powerful not only for their configurations and the acts that took place there, but also because the stones themselves are often elders of the land.

To find the elders of your land, simply consider what around you has been there the longest. It may be the mountain itself that you live on, the river nearby, or the desert you live in. Likely there will be many elders, some older than others.

The land is certainly not unchanging. Land spirits notice the shifts around us, especially those made by humans. Just because a land is changed doesn't mean the spirits aren't still there; their homes simply look different. Even in an industrialized mountain, the land spirit is there. If the river is flowing out of sight beneath the city, the land spirit is still there. But when a piece of land is unchanged, when it's an elder, the land spirits are more present because it is familiar to them. Although land spirits are very different from us, we can relate to them in this aspect: the familiar is more comfortable to be around, and so these places tend to be the best places to meet land spirits directly.

Guardians of the Land Spirits

Many of us don't live on land that is directly accessible in its unspoiled, ancient form. If you live in a city or any developed area, there might not be any uninhibited wildlife near you. But there will be a guardian. Guardians are natural features of the landscape that serve as protectors of the land and can grant you access, like a portal, to the land spirits.

Guardians can be old trees, boulders, small cave-like openings in the earth, creeks, hills, or ponds, to share some examples, but this list is by no means exhaustive. An elder is a place on the land where connection to the land spirits is more easily found. A guardian is an individual spirit that can help you connect to land spirits. Guardians are more common spirits to be found in the land because they are smaller. You might not live near an elder, but you certainly have a guardian. Guardians are often trees or boulders, familiar staples in the landscape that have been witness and party to the land spirits for a long time. The longer something has existed on that land, the closer its connection to the land spirits will be.

All guardians are hotspots for spirits of the land such as fae or nymphs, and elementals may be easier to call there too because they are such spiritually activated places. If your guardian is a tree, the dryad, a nymph that is the spirit of that tree, is the spirit that acts as the guardian. All those spirits coexisting is a beacon for others to join them, including you! They act as portals for land connection, by which I mean that reaching out to the land spirits there, and doing magic in general, is easier.

Guardian spirits can be playful, and I believe this is where the belief that faeries are tricksters comes from. If you don't approach with reverence, you might get messed with a little bit! But if you do bring an offering and take time to listen for their consent to the magic you plan on engaging them in, they are your greatest ally.

Guardians are gatekeepers for the land spirits and the main way many of us will converse with land spirits. You might live in the city and only have limited access to nature, and that is fine. Even having only one tree nearby is an opportunity to build a very poignant, personal relationship with a very powerful spirit.

Area of Reach

Land spirits in natural places have an "area of effect" in terms of their reach and influence. These are some common elders you may encounter and might try to connect with through the guardians near you.

Rivers

Rivers are extremely far-reaching land spirits. For example, let's look at a case study: the Susquehanna River or, as I refer to her, Mother Susquehanna.

Susquehanna State Park is in Maryland, spanning over 2,000 acres, where the Susquehanna River ends. However, Mother Susquehanna, the river itself, is 444 miles long with a basin size of 27,500 square miles. She is the longest river on the East Coast, spanning from New York, through Pennsylvania, and into Maryland.[5] The river covers more than half the state of Pennsylvania, greatly influencing the spiritual energy of multiple counties.

The energy of Mother Susquehanna is a land spirit that can be found strongly across much of this region, along the river's borders, and into the watershed: the places like cities, towns, and farms that benefit from her water.

---

5. "Paddle the Susquehanna," US National Park Service, last updated September 1, 2022, https://www.nps.gov/thingstodo/paddle-the-susquehanna.htm.

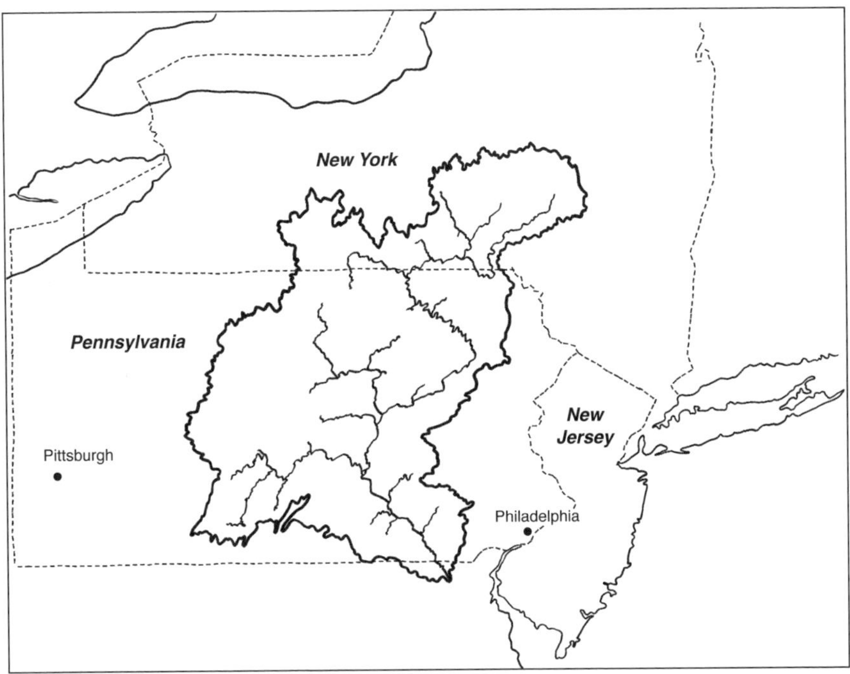

Map of the Susquehanna

This far-reaching area of effect means that all the places within the outline have a layer of energy in common: the spirit of Mother Susquehanna.

There are many land spirits found along her borders, as well. Let's return to Susquehanna State Park. This is where the river ends, in Havre de Grace, Maryland. I've found particular spirits of place there that are gateways to the land spirits. For example, in the state park itself, there is a large vulture population that serves as the vassals of the land. There are also guardians, prehistoric boulders lining the edge of the mountain and overlooking where Mother Susquehanna ends by flowing into the Chesapeake Bay. The boulders, like all guardians, protect the larger land spirit they share land with (in this case, the river).

In every respect, the river is a land spirit that is powerful to tap into for magical rituals done for releasing, particularly the kind of releasing we can do to accept the natural end that some situations and relationships must come to. The spirits of its land assist. The boulders, moved there by glaciers millennia ago, have a grounded, primordial energy of settling and stability.

The resident vultures, as carrion birds, have a natural comfort with death. These spirits coalesce to match the essence of the great land spirit: Mother Susquehanna's natural ending.

Along the Susquehanna, as it flows down through Pennsylvania, there are very different guardians, vassals, and other spirits, and these places all have different feelings to them. At some, bald eagles make their nests; at others, ancient petroglyphs have been found, indicating a sacred purpose for the Native American tribes that made their homes there in the past.[6] Each lookout and hiking trail has its own individual spirit. But at each of these points, the comforting, quiet, grandmotherly energy of Mother Susquehanna presides as well. Her area of reach, as a river flowing far and wide, is significantly larger than, say, a particular forest.

In India, the Ganges River is known as Mother Ganga, one of the three mothers of all Hindus.[7] In the most ancient sacred text of Hinduism, the *Rigveda*, she is said to be a goddess brought down from the heavens by the god Vishnu, the "Great Maintainer" of life, who promised that in exchange for her giving the waters of life to the humans, she would always be revered as one of the mothers.[8] She is still honored in India, where Hinduism, a polytheistic religion, is the majority religion even to this day. In Vishnu's city of Varanasi where Hindu death rites and birth rites take place, Mother Ganga receives humans at the end of their lives and welcomes them into their new lives.

The energy of Varanasi is more palpably Mother Ganga's than Vishnu's, for whom the city is named. The Ganges River floods the land each autumn due to a number of climate change and pollution-related factors.[9] To someone present during the worst of the flooding, it felt like a sad

---

6. "Petroglyphs of Pennsylvania," Pennsylvania Historical & Museum Commission Pennsylvania Archaeology, September 5, 2015, https://www.phmc.state.pa.us/portal/communities/archaeology/native-american/petroglyphs.html.

7. *Rigveda*, in *The Hymns of the Rigveda*, translated by Ralph T. H. Griffith (Motilal Banarsidass, 1973), 7.45.31.

8. *Rigveda*, 7.45.31.

9. P. G. Whitehead et al., "Impacts of Climate Change and Socio-Economic Scenarios on Flow and Water Quality of the Ganges, Brahmaputra and Meghna (GBM) River Systems," *Environmental Science: Processes & Impacts* 17, no. 6 (2015): 1057–69, doi:10.1039/C4EM00619D.

reminder that even if we revere our land spirits, as the people of India do, responding to their needs is an important part (perhaps the most important part) of living in right relationship with the land.

In Greece, the Potamoi are the river gods; rivers still bear their individual names, and the word *potamoi* is used to mean "river" in modern Greek as well. Where I live in Greece, Artemis's ancient temple is at a liminal space where seawater meets a river and turns to fresh water, evoking the flow of both the river spirits and the sea. There is river reverence in many cultures, and this is not an accident. Beyond the life-giving properties of water, rivers are very present, active land spirits, waiting to connect with you.

Exercise: FINDING YOUR ELDER: RIVERS

One important elder to recognize is your local water source. Rivers are critical elders. They are integral to life, and sacred in every culture. They are mostly permanent, even if their levels, lengths, or directions shift over time, making them truly elder among the land spirits. What is the river that your water flows from? Is there a creek first? What is it called? Doing this research grounds and connects you to your land in logical ways as well as spiritual. Record your findings in your land spirits journal.

Springs and Lakes

Springs and lakes are elder places of the land that also serve as guardians. There are specific nymphs in ancient Greek lore that are found in springs (*pygaeae* and the lesser-known *crinaeae*) and lakes (*limnades*).[10] These are all kinds of naiads, minor goddesses who preside over a specific freshwater source. The nymphs blur the line between elementals and land spirits or even fae, because of their dominion over a particular element. I have learned to see them as the land spirit of that particular place. A spring's nymph will both guard and embody its magic: when you visit a spring and call on the land spirits there, this is who you're talking to.

---

10. Pausanias, *Pausanias's Description of Greece*, trans. and ed. J. G. Frazer, 6 vols. (Cambridge University Press, 2012), 6.22.7.

The actual spring they inhabit is guarded by the land spirit of the place the spring is found as well. So too with lakes. Lakes and springs are often surrounded by forests, mountainsides, and other elders that work together in harmony to protect the land they share.

Mountains

Mountains are large sacred places that act as their own land spirit, and they also contain many more land spirits within them. Mountains contain springs, lakes, and caves and often oversee rivers and the sea as well. As elders, they are powerful, steady presences of the land, and spending time on a particular mountain for particular healing or goals is a common thread in mythology. Mount Olympus is the home of the Olympian gods, and to me it is still a place of powerful manifestation. I recommend visiting there to connect more deeply with the gods, the cosmos, and the gifts of intuition and clarity on your path. Mount Pelion is a mountain in Greece where all the heroes of ancient Greece, from Hercules to Achilles, were said to be trained by the healer and warrior Chiron the centaur. Visiting here on a creative or business retreat is a great way to accomplish your goals and overcome your obstacles to achieving them.

Mountains are places where connecting to the primordial power of the earth is most accessible. Ground, center, and reframe your problems with mountain land spirits.

Deserts

Deserts have spirits of their own, and depending on the desert, the spirits might be the only thing you encounter there. I spent part of my childhood in Bahrain, a desert island in the Arabian Gulf. This desert was large, expansive, and mostly empty. There was a powerful guardian, however: the Tree of Life. A mysterious, 400-year-old tree growing in the middle of the empty desert, it is a mystery how it survives.[11] Even in a desert, you will find life to connect to. And the land spirit of the desert is a powerful place to connect with quiet, solitude, and the lessons of meditation.

---

11. "Tree of Life: Bahrain, Middle East," Lonely Planet, accessed September 6, 2024, https://www.lonelyplanet.com/bahrain/attractions/tree-of-life/a/poi-sig/1315762/361009.

Caves

Caves, as deep, mysterious places beneath the earth's surface, hold wisdom that can be quite advanced to experience. It is in caves that I have felt the oldest, most powerful land spirits. I visited the Corycian Cave, the cave on Mount Parnassus sacred to Pan.[12] There is a theory that this is where the Pythia, the Oracle of Delphi, originally sat. Delphi is on the exact opposite side of Mount Parnassus from the cave, so they do share the same spirit of the mountain; and the cave itself holds the spirit of Pan, so much so that as I drummed within its depths, goats and sheep, including two rams with impressive horns, came to the entrance, like Pan's own presence holding vigil. Caves are best for shadow work, rituals of rebirth, and deep meditation, and I recommend always bringing many offerings, as it is a place of deep work and reverence.

Glaciers

Glacier is one type of land spirit I have quite minimal experience with so far in my life. I have seen the Gorner Glacier, in Zermatt, Switzerland, but I was not prepared for the physical ascent to climb it. In fact, I was amazed that you could climb it. Glaciers are treacherous, especially in recent years due to climate change diminishing their size and creating crevasses that are often invisible until it's too late. Glaciers are powerful for conquering fears, and because there is little to no wildlife on many of them, they are very powerful for air magic: playing instruments, doing breathwork, vocal intoning, singing, or chanting. They are known for their echoes and far-traveling sound and can be a powerful tool in healing the throat chakra using the techniques described.

They also are known to sing. Scientists in Iceland recorded the voice of glaciers and their movements, and you can hear it at the link in this footnote.[13] These sounds are audible because of the near-complete silence of glaciers, and they are an important tool for scientists in understanding

---

12. Pausanias, *Pausanias's Description of Greece*, 10.32.2.

13. Ugo Nanni, "The Sounds of Kongsvegen Glacier," SoundCloud, accessed September 6, 2024, https://soundcloud.com/ugonanni/sets/the-sounds-of-kongsvegen-glacier.

what happens within and beneath the surface.[14] If caves are mysterious, glaciers are an entirely different level of mystery. I encourage you to experience a glacier for yourself and meet the land spirits there.

Forests

Of course, I would be remiss not to include forests. The most common place people think of when they want to connect to the land is visiting a forest. This makes sense because they are accessible in most places in the world. Forests are also filled with many spirits, including millions of plant spirits, so the chances of having a spiritual experience in a forest are high. Depending on its size, a forest could have dozens of land spirits, as springs, lakes, and even caves are found within some forests. Pay attention to how the land feels as you walk in the woods. Maybe a specific glen, hollow, dell, or other break in the forest has a special feeling. The ancient Greeks had dozens of words for the nymphs of particular places: *napaeae* for small valleys or dells, *alseids* for groves, or *oreads* for mountains and particular grottoes (small cave-like openings in a forest or mountain) are some examples. There are many layers to forests that could take lifetimes to experience, and any magic or meditation to engage in connection to the earth, for personal growth, for clarity on your spiritual path, or to manifest desires will be heightened by working in the forest.

Exercise: MEETING THE ELDERS AND GUARDIANS

Research the myths, legends, and history of people who have lived on your land. Knowing their history and the relationship they had with the land can show you the expectations of the land spirits, and any historical events should also point to the source of trauma that land is still experiencing. Simply doing this research is a strong show of dedication to your land.

14. Ugo Nanni, "Did You Know… That Glaciers Can Sing?" Cryospheric Sciences, European Geosciences Union, June 3, 2022, https://blogs.egu.eu/divisions/cr/2022/06/03/cryoseismology/.

When you did research on the spirits of place where you live, did you notice any physical or emotional sensations arise at certain stories, names, or events? Record them in your land spirits journal so you don't forget.

Go outside and meet the elders of your land. Where are you called to explore? When you step outside with the thoughts of who the guardians might be, what place comes to mind? Who is beckoning you to them? Let your feet wander and see if you aren't led straight to them. If you stay local, it will likely be a large tree or stone. If you're called to a peak or a forest, you might meet an elder at the source. Take time over the course of your work with this book to connect here more and more, deepening your relationship with the land spirits.

Name or No Name?

Land spirits don't usually have names. In my experience, chances are that even if their name is given to you, it's to make you more comfortable, not the other way around. If you can easily research the name for the land spirits in your area, that's great: that will give you a clue to what sort of relationships humans had with the land spirits in the past, especially if the name has an association with a particular animal or another location. This can be a confidence boost when reaching out by giving you some context for what to expect. You might not feel called to use their name, particularly if it was given by the Indigenous people on colonized land; but the context and knowledge of the history of the land spirits' relationship with humans is still beneficial to know.

Unnamed Land Spirits

The vast majority of land spirits don't have names, myths, or legends surrounding them. That doesn't mean those spirits are any less present. They'll simply require more trust: trust in the land to receive you, but also in your own ability to perceive spirits and build a connection with them.

In many places where written language came much later than the practices of land spirit work, there is a lack of names to be found. The most primordial, human-removed spirits are unnamed, but they are strongly felt in places that they occupy. You can still build relationships with them. You can reach out, leave offerings, tell them about your plans to add a water feature to the backyard. You will still feel their presence strongly. You can work with land spirits without a name, even though your previous experience with calling on spirits might make you feel like something is missing in your petition.

Exercise: PETITIONING THE UNNAMED LAND SPIRITS

Write a petition you can use for the nameless land spirits of your land. Traditionally, petitions are invocations in a ritual to invite the energy of a particular spirit to help you with a particular goal, spell, or ritual or to celebrate the full moon or Wheel of the Year with you. It's a love letter to the land spirits, essentially.

Make it personal to your space, mentioning the elders that are encompassed in your local bodies of water or any trees you have nearby—if you've been given a name or not, you can simply call on "the Oak of the East Porch" or "my friend the Oak," for example.

An example petition, using the wilds of Pennsylvania as an example, could begin like this:

> *Beautiful land of Pennsylvania, in the care of our Mother Susquehanna, I invite your calming, steadfast, nurturing energy to be with me today. Your waters, so blue and deep, express the depths of your wisdom. Like the snake, which represents fertility, you curve through the land, giving life to all. Home to vultures, eagles, beavers, deer, and many more creatures, your nurturing knows no bounds. When I am outside and feel the breeze on my face, your love and warmth for the creatures of this land fills me with peace, and I am grateful…*

You don't have to ask them for anything. In fact, you don't have to read it aloud to them either. But if you choose to, you can incorporate it with other rituals or meditations like the one at the end of this chapter.

But Do They Have to Have Names?

Names are an important part of magic not to be overlooked. In Celtic traditions, even cars and altar tables are given names; in British tradition, homes are named. If you feel having a name for the spirits of your land is important, you can work with your land spirits to come up with a name for your home and land. You can use this as you would with any deity name: write it in petitions, draw it into sigils, and invoke it in ritual. Remember, deities are misnamed or mispronounced all the time, but they'll still show up for you if you're respectful and your intentions are honorable. Land spirits will react the same way.

Names are not set in stone. Deities and land spirits change over time. Their energy is different, and so their name might change as well. Consider the way many witches are given magical names in initiation. We have changed; we've gone through an experience that allows us to grow and shed a skin that no longer serves us. Names can be a part of that shedding process.

Other times, the names might have power on their own, but the meanings might not be clear to us. For example, I grew up in the Brandywine Valley of Pennsylvania, the land of the Lenape tribes (called Algonquin by white people). They called the Brandywine River *Wawaset*, meaning "the settling place of the wild geese," but they also called it *Sittacunck* and *Tankopanican*, words that we don't know the translation of today.[15] Not only do we not know the languages of these Native American tribes, but we don't know the specific tribes to credit within the many grouped together as Lenape for giving us these terms.

Even though I wouldn't use these names in my spiritual practice out of respect for closed traditions, knowing these names brings me closer to

---

15. "About the Brandywine Valley," TheBrandywine.com, accessed March 12, 2025, http://www.thebrandywine.com/about/; "The Origins of Naming Wawaset," Locust Grove Schoolhouse, Pocopson Township Historical Committee, accessed April 17, 2025, http://locustgroveschoolhouse.org/articles/origins-naming-wawaset.

understanding the land I grew up on. It also gives me an indication that the geese were held sacred, and I choose to acknowledge that. When they fly overhead, I use it as a reminder to be present.

This is also an example of how names are never simple. Consider deities: there are many epithets, sometimes dozens, for the same deity. Artemis, for example, has many, many epithets. She is called *Artemis Melissa*, "goddess of the moon who relieves pain in childbirth," but she is also *Artemis Cnagia*, "protector of slaves," and *Artemis Aeginaia*, "huntress, wielder of the javelin."[16] She is equally all of these roles; so too the land spirits are varied and many-named. And epithets, as well as accounts of unverified personal gnosis (UPG), remind us that spirits change over time.

Research and Cultural Appropriation

In the United States, a common question I hear is whether it's acceptable to reach out to land spirits and other spirits of place, because they are honored and revered by Native Americans. The methods, incantations, rituals, or other techniques used by Indigenous peoples to reach out to land spirits are closed practices; performing those rituals outside of those cultures is cultural appropriation. However, the act of introducing yourself to and working with the spirits of land, including the land spirits, is not.

These spirits are not just residents, caretakers, and facilitators of the land: they are the land itself. They were on the land before you, before your ancestors, before any humans. Respecting nature and the land itself is the essence of a spiritual path that involves land spirits. With respect as a guide, remember that any magic you do, or any landscaping or home improvements, affect them. Reaching out to form a relationship and continuing that relationship by keeping them in the loop of your needs is the most respectful way to coexist.

One of the most respectful ways I've found is reaching out to the many spirits of the land to heal the land. The atrocities suffered by Indigenous people on the North American continent have left a lasting impression and distrust in the land spirits there. Compound that with centuries of slavery,

---

16. Pausanias, *Pausanias's Description of Greece*, 3.18.2.

the Civil War, and atrocities like nuclear testing or facility failures, such as at Three Mile Island on the Susquehanna River in Pennsylvania, and it's unsurprising that the land might feel distrustful to us. But that is all the more reason for you to reach out to the spirits.

Why should you allow the land to suffer longer if you can be a part of the change it needs to heal? We have the power as the current guests on that land to acknowledge that hurt and do what we can to alleviate it.

One of the most important ways we can honor land spirits is to know their history with humanity. Learn the names of the people who have loved them. You are the person who loves them now. Even if their name is different now or unknown, even if you are the only person you know who is connecting with the land intentionally. The history and depth of who your land spirits are is a mystery that, in the uncovering, becomes part of their magic.

Meditation: THE NAME OF THE LAND

This is a meditation in which you will request a name from your land spirits or find one together, if they've never had one. Start with the research that the exercises suggest. The name might be out there or recorded somewhere. Just like in college, showing up without doing the reading and then asking simple questions that you already should know the answer to is not the way to get on their good side. They aren't here to do the work for you. Showing up prepared is paramount to a good relationship with them. There's a good chance you won't find a specific name, but do the research first.

If the name you find is a name that you're uncomfortable using, ask the spirits if they'd like you to use a different name. There might be a translation or similar meaning—or more likely, the land spirit has evolved and is less comfortable with that name now than they were. In many cultures and spiritual traditions, as discussed in this chapter, names change with experiences. They'll direct you to the name they want you to call them.

This meditation may need to be repeated before a name is given or found, especially if you're new to working with your land spirits.

You may want to save this exercise for after you've built a stronger connection with the spirits of your land. In chapter 3, we'll talk more about reaching out to your local land spirits, so if you've never reached out before, waiting to read that chapter might give you more confidence for this conversation.

However, if you're new to land spirits work but do have a strong relationship with your land—if you garden or have animals that keep you outdoors a lot; if you've done ritual outside; if you choose native, bee-friendly plants and don't use harmful chemicals; or if you've simply lived there a long time—the land has already taken notice of you.

When you feel you know your land well enough to have this conversation of choosing a name, go outside and prepare to meditate to connect to the spirits of your land.

Materials Needed

Comfortable chair or cushion if needed
Offering for the land, such as a cup of unsweetened herbal tea

If you have already met the elder, go to that elder. If you have not, visit the oldest, biggest, or most private tree, creek, or boulder nearest your home.

When you're ready, sit comfortably and close your eyes. Take deep breaths, inhaling through your nose and exhaling through your mouth, if able. First, focus on the physical feelings of the space. What is the temperature, and how does that affect your body? Are you shivering? Sweating? Can you feel the warmth of the sun? The chill of a breeze? Bugs near your head?

Then move to your sense of smell. What are the scents rising up around you? Moss, dust, flowers, flowing water? Match those smells to the sounds you're hearing. Is there a rustle of a mammal in the bushes across the yard? Or a scurrying sound in the tree at your back?

Once you feel fully present in this landscape with all your senses, reach out to the land spirits. Use your will, your intuition—the part of yourself that comes alive in ritual, that you feel in meditations when you finally stop fidgeting. This is your spirit self. This is who the land spirits will communicate with.

You should feel the land spirits' presence when they answer your call. The energy will shift, and birds might stop singing, or winds might pick up—these are common experiences I've had when inviting the spirits of the sacred wild to commune with me.

Once you feel their presence, with your mind's voice, introduce yourself if they haven't met you before. Then simply ask them what they'd like to be called. Consider this akin to introducing yourself to your neighbors: be pleasant, amicable, and to the point. This is an example of a simple exchange you can have here: "I'm Elyse. Nice to meet you. I love living on your land and am grateful to be here and that you've taken the time to meet me today. What can I call you?" As you wait for your answer, stay tapped into the land: the sounds, the smells, the feel of wind, sun, rain, or other weather. This answer might come quickly, but more likely it'll take a few minutes of waiting.

If you're losing focus, ask a follow-up question: "I'd like a name to use to call upon you to properly offer you respect" or "For humans, names help us build relationships, and I'm eager to build a relationship with you." Once a name or a title is shared with you, open your eyes and leave your offering.

If you aren't given a name, try this meditation again at a later date after you've made more offerings and built a connection with the land.

If you're given an answer that isn't a name, such as "I have no name," "There is no name for me," or even a negative response or feeling like "I don't want to," then you might need to reevaluate your relationship to the land. Have you been using harmful chemicals on your land? Do you live in an HOA where they are using them? Do you have more invasive plants than native ones that are harming the ecosystem? Land spirits will want a clear accounting before they'll begin a relationship.

Once you've come to the end of your introduction and you've opened your eyes, leave your offering and take your time returning indoors. You might get an indication of the next step in your relationship with your land spirits. Sometimes they'll appear at this moment as a creature looking at you: don't be surprised if you find yourself having eye contact with a fox! You might hear birds resume singing or have a bee land next to you. These are all examples of the land spirits affirming the start of something beautiful.

CHAPTER 3

Building Relationship with the Land

The slightly unsettling reality of land spirits is that they've already been watching you. The land you grew up on watched you grow up there, and maybe there are fond memories of playing outside or engaging with nature that come to mind when you think of land spirits. The spirits of the land you live on now have taken notice of you from the time you moved that first box into your new home. This is a comfort, not a stressor, however. If you are seeking to live as strongly as possible in union with the land, they've taken notice and are already on your side. This doesn't mean you have to live off the grid or never buy plastic again. It simply means you've done your best to show respect to the land around you. This takes some reprogramming and attuning. I call this mindset and approach to life the path of the earth intuitive.

In this chapter, we'll look at what being an earth intuitive means and how you can begin building a relationship with the land through offerings, rituals, and mindfulness.

Becoming an Earth Intuitive

Becoming an earth intuitive is the first step to building a relationship with land spirits. Identifying as an earth intuitive means you are listening to the earth's needs and working to put the earth first in your decisions. If you never build an altar or invite the land spirits to your rituals, that's fine. You can still have a fulfilling relationship with them if you learn this one skill.

Opening up your intuition to their needs, learning to listen to the land with not just your senses but also your heart, and stopping to consider nature before you act in anything is the essence of this path. An earth intuitive notices when the plants need more or less water. They also feel the discomfort of plants in areas where they're exposed to toxic chemicals, like roadside planters or medians on highways. Earth intuition will tell you when the birds in your area are hot and need a birdbath. It'll guide you to the abandoned stray kittens in your neighbor's barn that no one else noticed were there.

In chapters 1 and 2, you learned about the land spirits around you, what to look for when it comes to land spirits, how to locate the spirits of place. This chapter is all about introducing yourself to the land spirits and giving them a chance to get to know you. A formal introduction is always a nice way to start. Introducing yourself is important because it shows respect for the land spirits as autonomous spirits, just as you would be sure to give your name to your human neighbors. Introductions are important too because they give you the chance to explain and assert your intentions for being on that land. They provide an opening for future communication and allyship.

Exercise: INTRODUCE YOURSELF

The land is aware of you, but a proper introduction is always nice. And remember that the land has been through suffering, whether that's the human-caused disasters, natural disasters, or human suffering that the land has witnessed. Keep this perspective always in your work with the spirits of place. They are wary of humans for very good reason. Showing you understand that is key in building trust. This petition can be said the first time you do the upcoming exercises, starting your day with the land spirits and grounding and centering with their help.

You should also mention the land spirits if they do have names, such as rivers or mountains you live near. Here's an example introduction:

> *Here in the crossroads of the spirits of the Brandywine River and the Schuylkill River, I beseech your love and ask for acceptance on your land. I thank you for your warm welcome and acknowledge the hurt done upon these lands and to the people who you welcomed in years past. Though I cannot undo the wrongdoings here, I am here to help and be at your service in the ways that I am able.*

Simple Connections

Land spirits don't require ceremony, bells and whistles, or any pomp and circumstance. Building a relationship with the land is about simple connections. They are there, watching and often protecting. When you consciously begin reaching out and spending time with them, this is the best way to deepen that relationship.

Once you've introduced yourself to them, daily communion with them is the next step in building a relationship. As the following sections explore, it's not about long periods of time spent together but frequent connection. Land spirits are also not the most concerned about action: rituals of connection can have simple intentions. They don't need you to only show up when things are hard or when you want to make change or perform magic. If you are showing up simply to say good morning, that is the right pace—work with the land spirits is about grounded, regular connection.

Exercise: START YOUR DAY WITH THE LAND SPIRITS

Starting your day with some sunlight and some fresh air is a gift to your health and a simple way to grow your relationship with land spirits. If you're already taking the time to have coffee at home, just take it outside. Consider brewing an unsweetened cup of herbal tea for the land spirits too, and once it's cooled to room temperature, pour it out on the ground in offering.

If you don't have time in the morning, try a cup of tea or glass of wine outside before bed. The liminal times of sunrise and sunset are great opportunities to meet with the land spirits.

Grounding with the Land Spirits

Grounding and centering is the first step to raising energy. It is how I recommend everyone start and end their day, and it is a tool to return to throughout your day as well. Simply put, grounding is connecting yourself to the earth, and centering is connecting yourself to your core. This "core" can be seen as your higher self, your inner voice, or your energy body. Being grounded and centered allows you to be present in the moment and feel your own energy clearly. Witches, pagans, Druids, and other spiritual practitioners do it before magical workings, meditations, or rituals because it allows you to be in the right headspace to set intentions and to notice and feel other spirits who want to reach out to you. The two practices are typically done together.

Grounding and centering might feel different for you. Dodie Graham McKay explains in *Earth Magic* that it feels like two spirals of light, one of the earth and the other of her heart space, meeting in the center of herself.[17] Your center might be different as well. Feel if your center is in your throat, in your solar plexus, or in your heart; for me, it is between my heart and throat, and when I am properly centered, it feels like a guitar string that is tightened and tuned. Maybe it's a glowing yellow or white light instead of green. Experiment with tweaking the visualization until it works for you.

If you are less visual, consider how it feels. Do your palms feel tingly when you've centered? Do the bottoms of your feet feel warm? Maybe your back straightens and you feel a tether to the earth. These are all indications that you're grounding and centering successfully.

---

17. Dodie Graham McKay, *Earth Magic* (Llewellyn Publications, 2021), 27.

Grounding and centering is also a great way to introduce the land spirits to your energy. It's actually quite an intimate practice, rooting yourself into the land. The more you ground and center with the land, the stronger your relationship with the land will be and the easier the practice of grounding will be too.

Grounding

There are any number of ways to ground, but the land spirits provide a unique opportunity to truly connect to the literal ground beneath you. What most people mean when they use the word *grounding* is to settle yourself, your intention, and to fully be present in the moment. *Earthing* is another word for this practice, a more direct way of suggesting connecting to the earth to settle your energy. Incorporating nature is an incredibly helpful way to do this, as it is always staying present. Remember that even indoors, you'll still connect to the land with grounding practice; there's just more in the way.

One easy way to stay grounded is to observe nature. Every day of autumn, the leaves on the trees are in a different chromatic flow. Every spring, the flowers array themselves in exciting mosaics of color and budding greenery that change almost by the hour. And summer and winter, often seen as static seasons when not much changes, are just quieter and slower about their changes. Plenty is changing; we just aren't often present enough to see those changes if we're not looking for them. Ask a gardener—they'll tell you the azaleas will come and go in late winter, the wisteria is a blink-and-you'll-miss-it early summer bloom, and the night-blooming flowers really find their streak in the height of summer. And even in the winter, watch for those snowdrops to blossom above the shelter of the dead leaves, the twiggy branches that begin to fall as they break and make way for budding branches, and the way the snow or sleet dresses up the trees. These are the daily changes we can tune in to. When we do, we can find ourselves staying present, and suddenly we're grounded.

Exercise: GROUNDING WITH THE LAND SPIRITS

Go outside, barefoot if possible. Stand or sit with your legs comfortably apart and your feet planted to the ground. Hold your hands open on either side of you, palms down to the ground.

Feel the solidity of your feet on the ground. Is the ground rocky or solid? Smooth, hot, cold? Feel it. Ask the land spirits to support you by sending a pulse of loving energy down through your feet and your palms.

Close your eyes and feel the strength of your legs extend through your feet. See this strength as roots. These roots are brown, healthy shoots, glowing a warm, earthy, mossy green color as they extend. See them strengthen with each extension beneath you, and feel that strength surge up into your legs, your torso, your neck, and up through your crown. Feel the warm green glow fill your body. Feel yourself connected to the earth.

Imagine the roots growing from your feet and down into the earth beneath you. If you're indoors, see those roots extend deeper, past the layers of concrete, until they reach the soil.

When you feel yourself rooted, return your attention to the green glow in your body. Follow it up to your heart space, and feel its warmth there. This is your center. Let it radiate from you, pulsing up to your throat and down to your solar plexus. With each inhale, let it glow stronger. With each exhale, feel your roots extend and deepen into the earth beneath you.

This may take more time the first few times, but it gets easier with each repetition. When you feel centered and grounded, send another pulse of love from your feet down to the land spirits in gratitude.

Centering

Centering is best done after grounding. Once you feel connected and grounded to the earth, bring your attention to your body, mind, and the work at hand. Centering yourself is about focusing your intention. If you're grounding and centering simply to begin your day, your intention can be a focusing of your mind on what lies ahead, such as "staying positive about the new system we're implementing at work." If you're grounding and centering in preparation for a wider ritual, assert the intention of that ritual. Grounding brings in the calm energy, and centering focuses it where it is most needed.

Exercise: CENTERING YOUR ENERGY

This is a visualization best performed directly following the grounding exercise. With your energetic roots connected to the earth below you, allowing that circulation of energy to flow through you, let your mind think through all the tasks ahead of you. As you do, allow yourself to form an intention. It can be as specific as it needs to be for what is to come, such as "May my presentation go smoothly," or more general, such as, "May I be met with kindness as I go about my day." Send this intention down through your roots. It will start in your heart chakra, radiating down to your solar plexus and then down along your roots to the earth. Feel it reach the earth, and feel the earth receive it with a gentle, warm glow. In return, send gratitude to the earth for receiving your intention. When you feel that the earth has fully received your intention and your gratitude, push your palms down to the earth in a final farewell before rising. As you go about your day, tap back into your rooted connection to the earth by opening your palms or pushing your feet against the floor of the ground and feeling for your roots. With practice, you'll feel the roots rise to meet you quicker and quicker. No matter how industrial or indoorsy your life is, the earth will rise to meet you.

Offerings to the Land

Sacred reciprocity is a key facet of healthy relationships with land spirits. Leaving offerings for the land spirits is a great way to build relationships with them, and in return, land spirits will also leave you offerings. Through this simple practice, land spirits will become part of your spirit team, and you will feel more confident and supported by their presence in your magic and rituals.

Here are the types of offerings you can leave land spirits:

First Fruits of Your Harvest

First fruits are a very ancient offering to land spirits. When you harvest from your herbs in the windowsill or the tomatoes in your garden or even cut flowers for a bouquet, give the first ones that you harvest to the land spirits. These first fruits can be placed on your altar, if you keep one, and can serve as an offering to your deities or ancestors if that feels appropriate for your relationship with them. They can be offered directly to the land spirits by being left on the vine in your garden or placed at a nearby tree line where it will be safe for animals to come and eat them. First fruits are an offering common across many cultures, including ancient Hebrew, Roman, and Greek traditions and even modern Kwanzaa celebrations—*Kwanzaa* means "first fruits" in Swahili.[18] Here in Greece, they're left on springs in villages, as springs are thought to be the home base for the land spirits of the village.

Libations and Food Offerings

A cup of cooled, unsweetened herbal tea is a powerful offering not only of water, the lifeblood of nature, but also the plant spirit you've chosen for the tea. Pouring this out for the elder or guardian of your land is a wonderful offering. Making offerings part of your daily routine, especially alongside the earlier exercises for starting your morning with the land spirits, grounding, and centering, is a sure way to grow your relationship with the land.

Other food offerings are based on location. These are offerings the land spirits might be accustomed to over time or that have an egregore of their own associated with their significance and power. Here are some examples of offerings based on location:

---

18. Carolyn Otto, *Celebrate Kwanzaa: With Candles, Community, and the Fruits of the Harvest* (National Geographic, 2017), 3.

- Corn and tobacco for North America
- Cream or milk and honey for Britain and Ireland
- Oranges for the Mediterranean
- Potatoes and local cheeses for central Europe

Research the crops that are indigenous in your area and try offering these to see how well they're received.

Offerings to Emissaries and Vassals

The animals of our land are often the strongest spirits of place to connect with. Feeding them is an offering to the land that encourages connection with these emissaries, and it certainly curries favor with the land spirits they represent. If the vassals or emissaries are birds, having a bird feeder is an excellent offering. Be sure that what you're feeding them is healthy, and be aware of any illnesses present in your area that might infect the local bird population if they congregate at your feeder. Red-dyed hummingbird food has been shown to cause tumors, for example.[19]

Deer are vassals of the woods behind my home in Pennsylvania. I leave offerings of asparagus, broccoli, carrots, and other vegetables that are safe for them to eat. Remember that pollinator species are opportunities to care for the land. And when growing tasty treats for nature, consider the importance of native plants that their diet is meant to consist of. Where I stay when I'm in the US, we are in the process of ripping out all our grass and replacing it with native clover for the bees to enjoy. In Greece where I live, I have several feeders for the cat colony I care for—and the vet visits and flea and worm treatment ampules I administer are also offerings to the land in my mind. If you build a bat house in your trees, this is an excellent offering to the land. Anything you do to care for the animals of your land is an offering.

---

19. "No Red Dye," Journey North, Arboretum at the University of Wisconsin–Madison, April 29, 2015, https://journeynorth.org/tm/humm/food_red_dye.html.

Hair

Hair is my favorite offering to spirits of all kinds. Hair is the strongest, deepest, most intricately "us" part of us. It's with us for a very long time, usually, especially from our head. And it holds our DNA and a record of our past that isn't found in other places in our body (except bones, but you'll probably want to leave with all the bones you came with). When you're on a hike and feeling grateful for the experience, offering a hair onto a tree you pass is a great sign of respect. Hair is our purest form of self. It is with us for many years, and it literally emerges from our crown chakra, sacral chakra, and other chakra centers. Offering this essence of self builds a strong connection with the land spirits.

I don't recommend offering hair anywhere you're on the fence about. Be sure to only offer it if you are comfortable with the energy of a space and if you are willing to leave a part of yourself there, because that's what hair is.

Exercise: OFFERING HAIR

There are innumerable ways to offer hair, but this is one ritual I do near the spring equinox as a way to welcome back the birds from their migration. Start collecting your hair from your brush each morning in a jar. On or around the equinox, or when birds are beginning to make their nests in your area, release the hair to the land spirits for the birds to use in their nests. If you can't or prefer not to keep a jar of hair, you can do it in the morning when you connect with the land spirits instead. Bring the hair outside with your morning coffee and release it to the land spirits. I also bury hair in my plants as fertilizer.

Offerings of Service

Perhaps the most important thing we can do for the land is offer what it needs. This is why your daily communion with the land is important: you're opening the dialogue to hear what the land spirits need. Changing the dirt in your potted plants; feeding them nutrients and natural fertilizers;

removing waste, rubbish, and debris from gardens and growing plants; and planting native plants are all ways to offer service to your land spirits.

You can also look for opportunities to advocate for the land, including volunteering for waste cleanup initiatives and looking for ecoactivism causes to donate time and money to. Tell the land spirits of your home that you've donated money in their name when you have your morning check-in with them. They will be grateful.

Offerings of Voice and Music

Music has been used throughout history for spiritual rituals and communion. When I lived in Baltimore, there was a small human-made waterfall placed in a creek. I would step out into the middle of the stream, sit on a dry rock, and sing. No one but the land and river spirits could hear me, and it grew our relationship so beautifully.

Now, in Greece, I sing and drum to the sea and land spirits, sitting on the liminal rocky shore as close to the water as I can. I like to let them guide me in the notes and tones they want to hear, but you can also practice a song if that feels more comfortable. You also don't have to sing to offer your voice. The land does not require talent, but if singing is too far out of your comfort zone, try chanting, intoning, or simply talking instead.

Incense Offerings

Incense is plant materials that are burned to create fragrance or clear or cleanse the energy of a space, and when it is lit with intention, it is a powerful offering. Incense is also connected to almost every element, as it is made of plants, connecting it with earth; when lit, of course it invokes fire; and air is connected to incense through its smoke. If you live somewhere safe to offer incense outdoors, I recommend Tibetan rope incense, as it burns cleanly, leaves no trace, and burns quickly. Never leave anything burning unattended, and dispose of waste properly. Wildfires are a risk where I live for much of the year, so I don't often offer incense outdoors.

You can also create loose incense using plants from your land. This is a fantastic offering to burn on your land spirits altar indoors, which we'll discuss later in this chapter.

Other Types of Offerings

This is by no means an exhaustive list of offerings. As your relationship with your land spirits grows, so too will your understanding of their preferences. H. Byron Ballard, an author and community leader in Appalachian folk magic, shared on my podcast that the land spirits of Appalachia love the stickiest, sweetest, most brightly colored candies you can find![20] She also offers soda or other sugary drinks.

Sugar, particularly honey, has some historical precedent as an offering. Honey is an offering recommended in Irish and other Celtic-inspired traditions, especially combined with cream.[21] This is another offering I'd recommend trying especially if you live in Celtic lands or feel a draw to honoring those traditions.

I also have found that some land spirits enjoy shiny things. Coins and bits of foil (especially if you can do origami and fold it into something beautiful) were favored gifts of my land spirits in Baltimore. And olive oil is another favored offering, particularly in Hellenic (Greek) polytheism and for gods of the Hellenic pantheon. If you get the inclination to leave something as an offering and it isn't harmful, give it a try. Chances are this is the land communicating its wishes to you.

Offerings can be an isolated activity or part of a wider ritual. I find myself leaving offerings much more than I do any magic with the land. Remember that the most important offering to the land is your time. Spending time outside and with your land spirits is a great way to guarantee they're open to a relationship. Proving you're here to help is sometimes as simple as showing up ready to listen.

Exercise: REGULAR OFFERINGS TO THE LAND

Begin a regular practice of leaving offerings or completing offerings of service. If you're a gardener, that can be you offering your time to

---

20. Leandra Witchwood and Elyse Welles, hosts, *The Magick Kitchen Podcast*, season 7, episode 9, "Community Mindsets Rooted in Simple, 'Small' Magic: The Lessons of Appalachian Folk Practice with Byron Ballard," April 8, 2024, https://www.themagickkitchen.com/podcast/.

21. Jane Wilde, *Ancient Legends, Mystic Charms, and Superstitions of Ireland* (Boston: Ticknor and Company, 1888), 261.

the land. If you volunteer with your community, there's your offering. If you walk in the park, pick up some trash. And make a conscious effort to listen to the land for what it needs. It will guide you to what you can do.

Gifts from the Land

As your relationship deepens with the land spirits, you will find that the land honors that sacred reciprocity by giving you gifts in return. I find that these simple exchanges become a form of communication the land can have with you. It becomes a way for the land to make itself heard and know that you are listening.

Gifts from the land include anything natural you are guided to take. When I was filming a lesson for my online community, I wanted to talk about different ways to use wands. I went to a field near my home, and I shared with the land spirits that I didn't have the right tools to demonstrate all the kinds of wands, stangs, staffs, and more that you can have. They guided me to several fallen branches that I could use. I left my hair in gratitude and left the sticks as well after filming was finished.

Sometimes they'll offer instant acknowledgment of your offering. In Baltimore, the guardians of my apartment complex were three maple trees. One of them overlooked my balcony. When I would leave offerings on my land spirits altar, little helicopter maple seeds would fall on me, sometimes right on the altar. These little acknowledgments are expressions of love and appreciation.

If you're given a gift by nature, such as a feather or a stone or even an old animal skull, offering hair is my favorite way to say thank you. For big gifts like animal bones, I usually go back to the spot with an herbal tea or simple cup of water that the land can enjoy as an additional offering, in gratitude for such a powerful gift. If you're taking gifts from the space, you also should feel comfortable with that decision being sanctioned by the spirits of the land there. They'll let you know with unsettling feelings and even darkening clouds and heavy winds if they don't want you to take it. A good rule of thumb is to hesitate a minute and check in with the land before accepting what you are perceiving as a gift. Hover your hand over the item, and if you feel a bit of magnetic pull to take it, then great. If there's a bit of resistance, it is best to leave it. Always be mindful of laws and what is best for nature: check for posted signs, and particularly with seashells, make sure it won't hurt the ecosystem to remove them.

As your relationship with the land spirits grows, you may be guided to ask their help for ancestor work, deity work, or magical workings. A great way to get them involved is to ask them for a stone, herb, or other ingredient they'd want you to include. If you know you need a feather, a pinecone, or another specific natural element for a working, ask them. Asking for gifts in return is an important part of the reciprocal relationship with land spirits.

Exercise: KEEP A RECORD OF OFFERINGS AND GIFTS

Keep a log of what you've offered and how it was received, as well as what you've been given and what you offered in return. This is not meant to be overwhelming but to draw your attention to the progress of your relationship with land spirits.

A simple notation without details is fine. For example: "8/9/24–Received white quartz stone. Gave chamomile tea." This will help you learn what your local land spirits most enjoy and what they like to give you.

Creating a Land Spirits Altar

A land spirits altar is a space created in your home or outside of it for connection to the land spirits. I recommend inviting them to create it with you. This is a place where you can regularly commune with the land, leave offerings, meditate, bless or consecrate items, journal, and do anything else you'd want to invite the land spirits to be a part of.

I do not own my own land or even have a balcony of my own, so my land spirits altar is indoors. I use a small bowl that I refresh with gifts I am given on my walks around local land. I've had in it things like pinecones that nearly fall on my head or fallen leaves. Hibiscus, jasmine, geranium, and rose grow wild near me, so when I find fallen flowers, I like to bring them home for my land spirits altar as well.

I keep this bowl on my main altar as a reminder of the land around me that nourishes my spiritual practice. When I want to make offerings to the land, I take them outside to a nearby field, the coastline of the sea, or to my nearest guardian, an ancient Greek pine tree at the end of my street.

If you do have a space outdoors that you can connect to regularly, I recommend having an outdoor altar. When I lived in Baltimore, I had a flat-top candleholder that I found at the thrift store that served as my land spirits altar. It was wrought iron with oak leaves and acorns adorning it, which spoke right to my soul. It was a space to connect me to nature at the end of each workday.

My outdoor altar was very simple, but you could of course create a bigger altar with more intentional purpose. Have a statue of Gaia, a Green Man, or another earth-based deity or spirit that speaks to you. Walk around your local land and ask what wants to be included on your altar. Just as I recommended, taking a moment and pausing to feel the energy of items to see if you can take them home, hover your hand over the item that drew your attention and ask if it wants to be included on your altar. If something beautifully clear happens, like a leaf gets stuck in your hair or an acorn falls right on your head, it's likely that these items are most keen to be included in your altar!

Your outdoor altar might evolve into a place of communion with the other spirits of place too. Hanging bird feeders or a bat house is a way to honor the emissaries and call them into your sacred wild.

Exercise: CREATE A LAND SPIRITS ALTAR

Decide first if you will create one indoors or outside. Find a vessel or platform you will use as the base of your altar, such as a bowl, a table, a candleholder, a tray, or a box. If you'll be creating one indoors, it can be part of your current altar, like mine as a bowl on my main altar, but it can also be by a window where you can better connect it to the outdoors.

If you're making an outdoor altar, go to the elder or guardian, if you have one on your land, where the altar won't be removed or disturbed, and ask if you can build one there. If there is no guardian,

I recommend a tree or particular place you like spending the most time, such as your porch. Dodie Graham McKay explains in her book *Earth Magic* that she has a wide, flat stone resting at the base of an old tree that she leaves offerings and pours out libations on—this is a great idea.[22]

As time goes on, refresh and add to your land spirits altar. Ideally, it should have all natural ingredients, so when you feel their energy is finished being a part of your altar, return them to nature.

Listening to the Land

Building relationships with land spirits is a ritual on its own, but we will now begin looking at the deeper ways land spirits can show up as allies in our spiritual practice. As you embark on your journey as an earth intuitive by leaving offerings, grounding and centering, and connecting more regularly and intentionally with land spirits, remember that the core principle behind all these practices is listening. When you listen to the land, you invite the sacred wild.

Ritual: CONNECTION WITH LAND SPIRITS

Bring an offering of your choice outside to a place in nature. I suggest going to the elder you connected with in the previous chapter's meditation. There are no candles or fuss for this ritual: just connection. The essence of land spirits work is simplicity. Use this time with land spirits to give your inner child time to have fun in nature and sit down to a picnic together.

Materials Needed

Offering for the land spirits
Something for yourself to eat or drink
Blankets, cushions, chairs, or anything you need to be comfortable

---

22. McKay, *Earth Magic*, 98.

Preparation

Read through the spell first. You may need to research the names of bodies of water, birds around you, or the nearest national parks or mountains. You also may want to bring a craft to do or a book to read if you want to spend more time in nature after the ritual.

When you're ready, get comfortable in the place you will do your working. Lay out your blanket, place your offering for them, and gather your portion for yourself. Once you feel ready, stand if able.

Directions

1. Call in the elementals of air. Say, "Spirits of the air, [name birds or winged creatures in your neighborhood], I embrace your energies of new beginnings, in my connection with the land spirits. Hail and welcome."
2. Call in the elementals of fire. Say, "Spirits of fire, great sun who watches us all, I invite your warmth and presence here. May you bring me passion and creativity in my connection with the land spirits. Hail and welcome."
3. Call in the elementals of water. Say, "Water spirits of [name your nearest body of water], I invite your [gentle/rocky, depending on the water near you] flow to guide me in love and laughter with your tides/onto your banks. Join me here in this space of connection to the land spirits. Hail and welcome."
4. Call in the elementals of earth. Say, "Land spirits of [name nearest mountains or national parks], I invite your frolicking nature to join me here. May your lessons of grounded joy guide me in connection to the land spirits."
5. When you feel their presence around you, pick up your offering to the land spirits. Hold it aloft and call on the land spirits. Say, "Land spirits, spirits of my home, I ask your presence here today. May this be the start of a beautiful relationship. May I always serve your highest good. Hail and welcome."

6. Pour out or otherwise place the offering for the land spirits to enjoy.
7. Sit down and enjoy your snack or drink.
8. While enjoying your drink, give gratitude for your land. The water that we too are made of. The sun that gives us warmth and comfort. The earth that gives us shelter and food. The air that gives us life.

There's no need to dismiss the land spirits when you're finished: it's their land! Just enjoy your time in nature. Take a nap or meditate if it's safe. Get some fresh air for as long as you can. When you're ready to leave, give your offering to nature safely and leave no trace of any litter.

During this ritual, especially as you stand to leave, look for any gifts nature is giving you in return. If you're gifted a pinecone, rock, feather, or pressable flower, add this to your land spirits altar.

CHAPTER 4

Protection Magic

Land spirits are your greatest allies for protection for two main reasons: they are already present in the land, and you are part of that land. Since these spirits are always present around us, they are the perfect spiritual allies to enlist as guardians of your family and your home. Any magic done to protect you, your home, your family, or your belongings will affect them. Remember that land spirits are the land itself; they are the foundation your home is built on. While we can intentionally invite them into our space in ritual or through meditation, we also must acknowledge, as I noted in the last chapter, that they're already here.

This is a blessing not to be taken for granted.

In a way, the land spirits already are protecting you, as they are protecting their land. You're protecting yourself as part of their space, and adding a layer of intention to what they're already doing.

Similar to the way I explained the importance of introducing yourself to the land spirits in earlier chapters, inviting them to join you in protection magic is equally as courteous. When you install protection magic like wards, shields, witch bottles, sigils, charged stones, or the like on your land, you're affecting the energy of the land spirits. It's only fair to give them a heads-up to what you're doing. And instead of just telling them ahead of time, or after the fact, you can invite them to contribute to the protective workings you're doing.

While land spirits don't take interest in the minutiae of your human goings-on, they do want you to be safe. You share a common interest when it comes to protection: they want their land to be safe above all else. So laying those protective barriers together is important. At the end of the chapter, you'll find an exercise to lay protective wards at your home with the aid of the local land spirits. Inviting them the way you would the elementals, your deities, or even your ancestors is a responsible thing to do for best results of any home protection magic.

Protection magic can be long term or short term. There's long-term protection magic, in which we place wards or blessed items to protect us or our home over time. These spells or workings might only be refreshed once a moon cycle, once a year, or never (or until you move). But there are also regular, repeated protection workings that land spirits can help you with, including preventative protection measures.

Energy Shielding with the Land Spirits

Shielding is the act of raising an energetic field around yourself to protect your energy from negative influences. Shielding is best done right after grounding and centering, as you're connected to your energy already and can draw up from the earth the shield you want.

You decide on the type of shield, and this can change day to day or even midday. A shield can be semipermeable to allow kindness and positive interactions to find you but not negative ones. This is my default shield because it keeps me open to connections that serve me, which is crucial to my business. I usually picture it as a bubble with a gentle green and pink sheen to it, like a bubble from a bubble wand.

If you're going into a crowded place, especially one that you know from past experiences is likely to affect you negatively, you might opt for an impermeable shield so no one talks to you or even notices you. Visualizing a brick wall or steel panels is a good option. I recommend using this solid type of shield for prisons, schools, festivals, concerts, or, if you're a country mouse like me, anytime you go into a city. You can also take a minute wherever you are and raise a brick shield anytime anxiety strikes.

If you're not a visual person, feel the way the energy of the land spirits meets your palms when you shield. This tingling warmth will be your sign that the shield is raised. I recommend shielding each morning when you ground and center outdoors with your land spirits.

Exercise: SHIELDING WITH THE LAND SPIRITS

Standing outside, barefoot if possible, place your hands out to your sides with palms spread, facing down to the ground.

Directions

1. Ground and center.
2. Once you feel the warmth of your center clearly, use your palms and your feet to draw up a shield from the earth. Visualize the energy of the earth traveling up the strong roots you've sent into the earth from your feet and radiating out to form a shield around your body.
3. When you feel a warm tingling rise into your palms, your shield is set. I like to press my palms against the shield up and around myself to remind myself it's there. You can do this exercise throughout the day as well, to remember the protection you carry with you from your land spirits.

Clearing and Cleansing

Clearing energy and cleansing energy are two different things. Simply put, clearing is removal, and cleansing is cleaning. Clearing is the removal of all energy and, for example, is useful for when you bring vintage items into your home and don't want their energy to be brought into your home and life. Clearing is also good for when someone unwanted has paid a visit to you or has been around you extensively, or when a deeply negative experience has transpired in your space or has happened to you. Cleansing is the energetic equivalent to mopping a floor or sanitizing your kitchen counters. It doesn't remove anything except the germs: the negative energy.

Clearing Energy

Clearings are finite removals of all energy. To clear energy is to remove negativity as well as the full energetic imprint. For example, after hosting a big party, the house retains a lingering energetic impression of the many people. It can feel a bit like static in the air, and can make focusing and relaxing difficult. Clearing that energy is always a good idea; not because anyone you had over was a negative influence, but because their energy simply needs to leave with them. Clearings can also be done for bigger issues, like refreshing your space after a breakup or when moving into a new home.

Clearings are a clean slate. They remove all energy from a space. This can leave you feeling pretty drained. Be sure to shield before clearing energy, and remember that because clearings are powerful and finite, they aren't required as often as cleansing.

Land spirits can't be cleared from your land accidentally. Even a powerful clearing, such as one to remove an unwanted house spirit, won't affect a land spirit. Perhaps if you wanted to keep them from your home's interior you could, with some powerful wards or personal shielding, but I don't know why you'd want to!

Exercise: CLEARING WITH THE LAND SPIRITS

Fire is a powerful aid in clearing because of its destructive capabilities. Be very safe with this working. If it is not safe to set a fire in your area, you can use an electric candle or visualization of flames instead.

Materials Needed

Lighter or matches to light your fire

Place to have a fire—firepit, chiminea, or a bonfire. If this is not possible, gather a cauldron or bowl in which you can safely burn resin or loose incense indoors.

Wood and kindling, if burning outdoors. If burning indoors, have a charcoal disk and tongs for the disk. Never light a charcoal disk with your bare hands.

Plant materia from your land (see preparation on the next page)

Bucket of water or sand in case of emergencies

Preparation

Gather plant materia from your yard that is safe to burn. Fallen pine needles, branches, twigs, or cuttings from yard work are great. Never burn fresh-cut plants or trees, as they are a challenge to burn and it is not as respectful to the land spirits. Be mindful that dried leaves create a lot of smoke that can be harmful with prolonged exposure. You can plan ahead and ask the land spirits' permission to cut some plants and dry them for this clearing ritual as well: sage, rosemary, bindweed, and mugwort are great allies in clearings.

If indoors, open all windows and doors. Secure pets safely in a specific room if needed, but have all doors open. This is important for the energy to clear.

Directions

1. If you are outdoors, use your matches and kindling to start your fire. If indoors, use your tongs to hold your charcoal disk to be lit by your lighter or matches. As the fire begins to catch, think about the energy that needs to be cleared from your home or the objects. Burn more plant materia as needed throughout the ritual to keep the flames lit and the smoke flowing.
2. Once the fire catches, stand if able and hold your palms out to the flame. Say, "Elementals of fire, I call on your powers of clearing."
3. Hold your palms down to the land. Say, "Land spirits of this place, I call on your protective powers."
4. State what needs to be cleared. Raise your palms between the fire and the sky, ushering the cleansing smoke to clear the negative energy and positive, to clear this place completely. Feel that energy flow up with the smoke into the aether.
5. For specific items that need clearing, pass them safely through the smoke. Be sure to keep them away from the direct flames. Always use caution around fire.

6. When the negative energy feels safely cleared, put out the fire safely and completely. Take a bit of the ash from the fire into your home. You can keep more of this ash for making black salt or adding to a witch bottle (both discussed later in the chapter).
7. Go to the hearth of your home with the ash. Think of the hearth as the heart of your home. This could be a literal fireplace, your living room, or the kitchen—wherever you spend the most time. Hold some ash on your palm saying: "All energy existing here. I release you. Energy, be cleared." Blow the ash toward the nearest open window or door. Repeat this in every room of your home that has a window.

Cleansing

Cleansing doesn't affect the presence of positive energy. Being mindful of when you choose to cleanse or clear is important. Let's say it wasn't a party that you hosted but an intervention hosted by your friends for you. You might not want to clear that energy, because the supportive love they promoted in that circle might be important for you. Cleansing might be a better choice in this case.

If you cleanse the energy around you, you won't lose your good mood—you'll actually improve it. Cleansing can be done daily in your space. If you have lots of people living in your home or have frequent guests, such as at a home office, this is a good idea, actually. Generally, each full moon (to rebalance the energy) or new moon (to banish negativity) is a good chance to refresh the energy. Cleansing also clears away stale energy, the cobweb-feeling energy that isn't serving anyone anymore. Think of this energy as the ash from spent incense: the magic was served; the ash is just what's left over. Removing that ash doesn't end the magic.

Cleansing a space is a great time to enlist land spirits. It is a teaching of Wicca and related modern witchcraft traditions that outdoor spaces don't need to be cleansed, because the land itself is cleansing. I have found this to be mostly true, the exceptions being places of heavy traffic, such as city parks or popular public areas, and places where great tragedy override the energy of the land spirits, such as battlefields or execution locations. As a rule, though, inviting the land spirits intentionally is a great way to invoke their protection more strongly. The land spirits are already there, cleansing the outdoor space simply with their presence, but they don't mind a little help.

It is not possible to over-cleanse or over-protect your space, unless you're using cleansings to replace the work you might need to do in order to make your space what it needs to be. It might become futile or even an empty gesture. While the cleansings would still "work," if you don't actually remove the people, items, or obligations from your mundane life that make your space energetically unhelpful or toxic, a cleansing is only so useful.

Exercise: CLEANSING WITH THE LAND SPIRITS

Just like clearings, cleansings are always best done with the help of land spirits. Invite them to participate in your working every time, and you will see the benefit. Salt is the ultimate essence of earth, but so is the dirt of your land. You will need dirt for this cleansing work. This might seem counterintuitive to use dirt to cleanse. Unless you have salt deposits on your land, dirt is the best essence of land spirits to embrace. You can do this in your home or on your person.

Materials Needed

Bowl for collecting dirt
Trowel or shovel to scoop dirt into bowl
Offering to the land spirits

Directions

1. Take the bowl and trowel to your land.
2. Ground and center with the land spirits.
3. Ask the land spirits for their aid in cleansing the space, and ask them to direct you to some dirt you can take inside. This can be done aloud or by sending the energy of the request into the ground beneath you as you ground and center.

4. Collect about a tablespoon of dirt; not much is needed. If you are on public land, be aware that taking soil from the public may be illegal where you live. Taking the barest pinch is the most I would recommend. You can also plan ahead and purchase potting soil that you leave in a pot outside on your land for a full moon cycle in order to acclimate it to your environment.
5. Leave your offering where you collected the dirt.
6. Sprinkle a small bit of dirt at the entrance to your home and say, "May no one enter here who brings ill intent to me, my family [say the names of those you live with], or this home. By the power of the land spirits, we are protected."
7. Enter your home and stand at the hearth. Sprinkle a small bit of dirt in the air around you toward the hearth (or throw it into your fireplace if you have a literal hearth) and say, "May love and laughter find us here. May fear and worry never come near. By the power of the land spirits, cleanse this space of negative energy."
8. Repeat step 7 while standing in the center of each room in your home. Repeat step 6 at the other doors to your home that people could enter through.
9. Return the bowl of remaining dirt to the hearth. This dirt will absorb negative energy, so return it back to the earth after a moon cycle. I recommend repeating this exercise on the new or full moon each month.

Baneful Magic

Clearings or cleansings can be paired with baneful workings in order to add layers of protection. Baneful means "poisonous; pernicious; destructive," and baneful magic is any magical action you take that encourages that.[23] This includes hexes, curses, bindings, and banishings. Here are brief

23. Noah Webster, *An American Dictionary of the English Language*, vol. 1 (New York: S. Converse, 1828), under "baneful."

definitions of these workings as per the teachings in my tradition, the eclectic Faery Tradition:

Jinx

A jinx is usually a light form of sending bad luck to a person, often conditional. For example, "If they leave me another voicemail, may they step in a puddle on their way into work."

Hexes, Reversals, or Crossings

These three terms—hex, reversal, and crossing—all define a short-term, specific negative effect directed at a person or situation, and they are often conditional. For example, "May any who enter this place feel unwelcome and leave quickly." Crossings are hexes that are triggered by a specific person crossing your path. Reversals, also called mirroring spells, are like booby traps. They are hexes that are triggered by a person sending you a curse or hex—so unless they instigate it, no harm comes to them.

Crossings, reversals or mirroring spells, and jinxes act as a tripwire for people: these workings are not taking away their free will but delivering a punishment if they use their free will to cross a particular boundary.

Curse

A curse is a long-term, specific negative effect directed at a person or situation. For example, "May all his business ventures fail and no one invest in him."

These are last-resort workings in the eclectic Faery Tradition, because they affect the will and quality of life of another person. If harm or destruction is aimed at another, it is baneful.

Banishing

Banishing is a reinforced shield against a particular person or a situation. This banishes, or removes them, from penetrating your energy physically, digitally, emotionally, or in any other way. For example, you might banish an ex from ever contacting or seeing you again.

Some people include banishing in the category of baneful magic, but I believe it is simply protective. When a banishing is done, no one is harmed; they are simply kept away from you. This makes banishings strong energy shields more than anything else.

Binding

Like with banishings, I do not include bindings in baneful magic, but many do. Bindings simply bind a person from affecting you in particular ways, without banishing the whole person. For example, you might bind your mother from commenting on your marriage or bind your family from finding your private social media profile. Some people even work bindings on themselves to quit smoking or other bad habits.

Banishings and bindings are often combined: for example, banishing an ex and binding them from contacting you. Remember to combine your magical workings with the necessary mundane actions. Blocking their social media accounts and phone number is part of the magic.

Grounding Negative Energy

As we explored in chapter 3, grounding and centering is a way of raising energy, but it can also be a tool to release negative energy. When we encounter challenges at work, experience negative interactions at the grocery store, or get overwhelmed with our responsibilities, these experiences compound and build up as negative energy that can be draining. It is a form of protection to release that into the earth.

When something threatens our energy and our well-being, we need to release the negative energy in order to protect them. This isn't the same as something outside of your comfort zone causing you to be challenged—we're talking about the real challenges that need to be overcome, like your child's bully at school, a crippling anxiety about asking for that promotion, a toxic coworker always being negative and critical, a nosy neighbor trying to convince you to spray your "weeds" for the millionth time, a parking ticket, and the like. These frustrations don't serve you, and so grounding them into the earth is a great way to release them and move on.

It is not selfish or harmful to release negative energy into the earth. The earth can handle anything that you need to release into it. Our human problems are just that: our lives are so brief and other to them, there's nothing we'd throw at our land spirits that they can't handle. Land spirits are connected to the earth as a whole, and when we release negative energy, we are allowing the energy to flow back to the earth. Our heartbreak, grief, confusion, or anxiety can't hurt the land spirits because they will simply transmute it back to neutral energy in the earth.

We recognize spirits in the land, but we can't project our human experience of being enspirited onto them. Grounding all your negative emotions into another person would be toxic and selfish, but doing so to the earth is natural. Especially when you're in right relationship with the land. You're not simply oversharing and never talking to these land spirits again. You're leaving offerings regularly, including them in the highs and lows of your life, and engaging them in protection magic. Grounding your negative energy won't hurt your relationship with the land or the land itself if you do it mindfully.

To do this, simply ground as described earlier, and then when you feel that connection of your soles and your soul to the earth, inhale the healing green energy of the land around you, and exhale the negative experiences, feelings, thoughts, and people you need to release. Repeat until you feel unburdened and leave an offering for your land spirits. An offering of service could work here too: do this grounding exercise right before gardening or yard work, or a walk around the block picking up litter.

Long-Term Protection

Wards, witch bottles, talismans, witch marks, and black salt are long-term protection measures that mark the land or your home as your own. They are ways of establishing boundaries, often at your actual property line, so that negative spirits, energy, or human influences are unable to enter your space. Since these are placed outdoors or at the entrance of the home, they are an opportunity to strengthen your connection to the land spirits.

These forms of protection work with the land and your intention to protect you and all who dwell in your home. I recommend getting a personal effect from each member of your home for any of these long-term protection measures. This can be hair, fingernails, a bit of breath, spit, or anything that is from the body. Some people include a photo of the family in their wards or witch bottles, but as you will not be unburying these items, that always struck me as too personal. Consider magical consent when building wards or witch bottles using personal effects of members of your home. Getting everyone involved by asking them to blow on the rocks before burying them or pull out a hair of their own to be buried with the rocks, for example, is a great way to ensure consent.

Wards

Wards are traditionally stones that are protective in nature, and many go with crystals like obsidian, black onyx, smoky quartz, or other stones that can transmute negative energy. But in my work with land spirits as protection allies, I recommend using stones that the land guides you to find. Burying these stones at the four directions of your home, resting them on a windowsill, or burying them at your front gate is a great way to protect your home. At the end of this chapter, the ritual working is a warding practice cooperating with your land spirits.

Witch Bottles

Witch bottles are singular wards, meaning instead of multiples needing to be placed at several points in the home or on the property to create a border or a grid of protection, they do all the protecting on their own.

Traditionally, they are bottles filled with personal effects of the people in the home, often including urine, hair, and fingernails.[24] They also usually contained sharp objects such as bent pins, rusty nails, or broken glass, to imply harm would come to those who brought negative energy to the home. Red thread is often found within or around witch bottles, as red is

---

24. Allison C. Meier, "Is There a Witch Bottle in Your House?" JSTOR Daily, May 13, 2019, https://daily.jstor.org/is-there-a-witch-bottle-in-your-house/.

the color of protection and thread is used to bind harm from coming to the home.

Because these are human-made objects that will remain in the ground for a very long time, be sure to use only natural, nonharmful ingredients like glass jars with cork lids. Always avoid plastic or anything that will poison the land when you're working with land spirits.

Exercise: WITCH BOTTLES WITH THE LAND SPIRITS

This witch bottle will be imbued with the power of your land spirits. You'll be inviting them to create the bottle with you and asking them to protect your home and family.

Materials Needed

Jar with a biodegradable lid, such as cork
Personal effects from all people and animals in your home
Bent pins or nails
Ash from a clearing ritual (optional)
Red thread (optional)

Preparation

Gather your family to participate, if they're willing, or ethically collect personal effects from everyone living in the home.

Directions

1. Take your ingredients to your outdoor land spirits altar or outside to the center of your property.
2. Hold the empty jar to the ground and say, "Land spirits of my home, I invite you to create this witch bottle. May it be a beacon of warning to all harmful energy, persons, or events not to affect us here."
3. When you feel the land spirits' presence, pinch a small bit of dirt from the ground and place it in the jar, saying, "The land is the foundation of protection. The land spirits are my guardians."

4. Put the personal effects in first, one at a time. For each, say, "Spirits of my land, please protect [name]."
5. Begin filling the jar with the other ingredients, repeating, "The land is the foundation of protection. The land spirits are my guardians."
6. When you seal the jar, say, "The spell is sealed."
7. Bury the bottle at your front gate, under your porch, or nearest to your front door as you can get while still being outside.

Black Salt

Black salt is a powerful tool for protection. In Western esoteric tradition, it is a salt made with ash or other black ingredients such as charcoal or iron filings. Some practitioners also add black pepper.

It is used to assert boundaries and protect those within its borders. For magical spells or rituals involving astral travel or mediumship, lying within a black salt circle is an extra layer of protection against unwanted spirits. It can also be added to witch bottles or wards' holes in the ground when you bury them.

Black salt is useful in a cleansing bath when you need to remove negative energy from your body, such as after interactions in negative spaces or with people who had negative energy. For binding or banishing work, black salt is a great ally.

Making black salt using ash from found materials on your land is a great way to involve the land spirits. You can also invite the land spirits when you place a black salt circle around your home. This is the most common use of black salt: pouring out a thin boundary line of black salt around your property's perimeter. Black salt can also be used at the doorway to your home or on windowsills to keep negative energy from entering. You may also choose to put some at the perimeter around your altar, especially if you fear someone with access to your altar is disapproving of your spiritual path.

Be mindful of the harmful effects salt can have on natural environments. A very thin border of black salt is all that is needed. The recipe that follows uses minimal salt out of respect for the land spirits.

Exercise: MAKING BLACK SALT WITH THE LAND SPIRITS

There are many ways to make black salt depending on tradition, but this recipe involves the land spirits. Don't worry if your black salt is more gray than black. If you want truly black salt, you can use a bit of charcoal to add color.

Materials Needed

¾ cup ashes (can be from a clearing, from your other rituals, or from your fire pit or grill)
¼ cup salt (local if possible, but any is fine)
Jar for the black salt
Pinch of dirt (to be collected from the ground during the ritual; see step 3)
Charcoal, black pepper, or iron filings (optional)

Note: If you do not have ash on hand and need to create some, only use found and natural debris such as fallen twigs or dried plant materia like pine needles.

Directions

1. Take the ash and salt outside to your land spirits altar, an elder, or a guardian.
2. Ground and center. Lift the jar to the altar, elder, or guardian and ask their blessing: "Land spirits of my home, I invite you to create this black salt. May it form a protective barrier from harmful energy, persons, or events."
3. When you feel the land spirits' presence, pinch a small bit of dirt from the ground and place it in the jar, saying, "The land is the foundation of protection. The land spirits are my guardians." If you are adding other ingredients, such as charcoal, black pepper, or iron filings, add them now. Any miniscule amount will add their energetic power of protection.

4. Fill the jar with the ash, saying, "May all harm directed toward me/my family burn away and turn to ash."
5. Add the salt, saying, "May all harm directed toward me/my family rebound from this salt and ground into the earth, harming none."
6. Close the jar and repeat the following three times, turning the jar counterclockwise (widdershins) each time: "Harm rebound."

This black salt can be stored for later use or used right away.

Witch Marks

Witch marks are sigils of protection drawn on your home with the intention that they will be permanent protection. Creating witch marks on your home is a powerful opportunity to invite the land spirits to protect your space.

Witch marks, also called apotropaic marks or protective marks, were found in homes, barns, churches, and other buildings throughout England for hundreds of years.[25] They are often carved into doors, in the ceilings of homes in roof beams, or under floorboards. The hearth was also a common place to find them. Today any or all of these locations are perfect for your witch mark.

Witch marks were meant to ward away any evil activity or energy from the home. They were very popular in the fifteenth and sixteenth centuries due to the witch trials rampant across England, hence their name.[26] These are some common witch marks:

Pentagram: A five-pointed star drawn in a circle was considered a symbol of virtue in the Middle Ages and was even painted on the shields of English knights.[27]

---

25. Brian Hoggard, "Protective Marks Lecture with Brian Hoggard," Churches Conservation Trust, May 27, 2020, YouTube, 33:21, https://www.youtube.com/watch?v=kHTG_xxpQzI.
26. Hoggard, "Protective Marks Lecture with Brian Hoggard."
27. Gerald Morgan, "The Significance of the Pentangle Symbolism in 'Sir Gawain and the Green Knight,'" *The Modern Language Review* 74, no. 4 (1979): 769, doi:10.2307/3728227.

Cross: As leaving marks was a folk practice during the Middle Ages, when Christianity reigned in England, the cross was seen as a protective symbol by many.

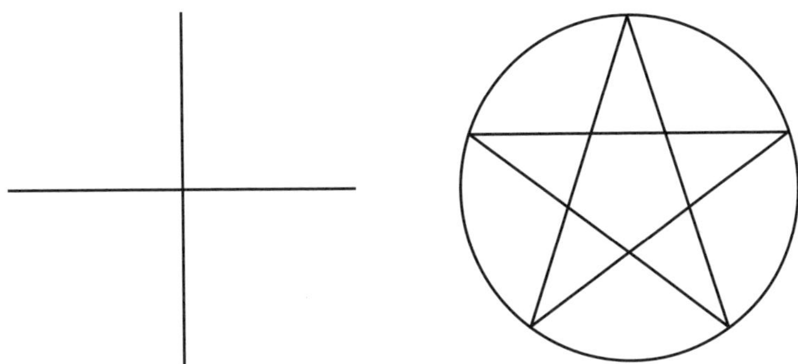

A Cross and a Pentagram

Daisy Wheels (Hexaforms): These are circular, complicated-looking geometric designs that were meant to confuse spirits. I've seen these on a tithe barn, a place where grain was collected from every farm in the village in medieval times. These barns were places where wealth was stored, and therefore protection from negative influence was extra important.

Hexaforms and Soot Ash in Somerset County, England

Marian Symbols: Simple shapes associated with the Virgin Mary, Jesus's mother, Marian symbols are created from two overlapping capital *V*s, like a *W*. They were common forms of protection. I saw one in a tithe barn in Somerset, UK.

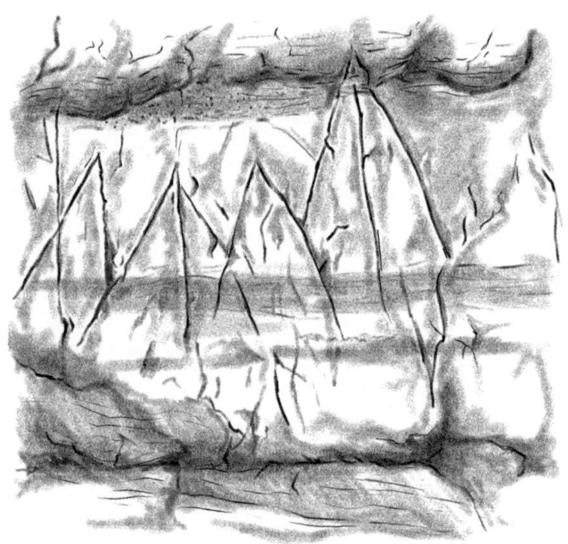

Marian Symbols in Somerset, UK

Burn Marks: Simply blessing a candle and creating a soot mark on the floor or door frame was another way of marking protection. A similar protection practice is found in Greek Orthodoxy, in which candles are brought home from the church on Good Friday, still lit, and that sacred flame is used to create a cross on doorways in and out of the home. You'll see this in the image with the daisy wheels found in a tithe barn in Somerset, UK.

Any of these symbols can be effective witch marks. You may also choose to create your own, using the following exercise, by inviting the land spirits to create one with you.

Exercise: CREATING YOUR WITCH MARK

Traditionally, witch marks were less personal and more cultural, as shown in the symbols explained previously. But creating a witch mark that involves the land spirits is a powerful way to amplify the protection. Consider combining the symbols on the list that speak to you with a personal symbol for your land. These are some ideas for symbols to incorporate:

- The imagery of your street name (especially if it is a flower, tree, or formation of land)
- The outline or shape of the elder or guardian of your space, such as a guardian tree with branches extending in a certain shape or a nearby mountain with a particular peak
- The silhouette of the skyline

Remember that witch marks are not about beauty or detail but about symbolism. If it speaks to you of the comforts of home and being surrounded by the land spirits you work with, it will do the job.

You can gently trace this witch mark onto the ground directly, or trace it with water from your hose onto the ground.

Talismans

Talismans are items worn or carried that are created and blessed with intentions of protection. While they can be recharged and blessed again and again, they don't need to be replaced, making them great protective allies for long-term safety.

Exercise: CREATING A LAND SPIRITS TALISMAN

Talismans can be anything, but for this exercise, you will be using a stone, an acorn, or another nut or seed from your land.

Materials Needed

White chime candle
Lighter
Stone, acorn, or seed that won't rot
Water from your land (from the tap is fine)
Small jar or cup that fits over the talisman

Directions

1. Take the ingredients to your land spirits altar. Ground and center. Tell the land spirits you are creating a protective talisman for yourself. Place all items on or in front of the altar.
2. Light the candle and call in the land spirits, saying, "Spirits of this land, I welcome you to this flame. Elementals of fire, I call your name. Be here now in blessing."
3. Dip the talisman object into the water three times, repeating each time, "Elementals of water, direction of flow, may negative energy to me never go."
4. If there is anything specific you wish to protect yourself from, such as a certain person or situation, state this. Pass the seed over the flame, safely so as not to burn yourself or the talisman, three times, repeating, "Elementals of fire, hear my charm. With this talisman, burn away all who seek to harm."
5. Hold the talisman to the ground, with your hands on top of it. Feel the land beneath your hands. Repeat three times: "Spirits of land, spirits of place. Keep those who wish harm away from my face!"
6. Allow the talisman to charge here with the land spirits for three days and three nights. Place the cup over it so it does not get disturbed or taken by other beings. You can also lightly bury the object for more safety. Make sure not to forget where it is buried!
7. Each day for three days, return to the talisman and repeat step 5, removing the cup so your hands have direct contact with the talisman.

When it is ready, start carrying your talisman with you every day, in your pocket, in your purse, in your car, or anywhere you know it'll travel with you; you don't have to see it for it to work. You can recharge the talisman by repeating step 5 or leaving it at your land spirits altar during a full moon.

Sacred Reciprocity

In this chapter, I've explained several of the best protective measures found across magical traditions around the world. All these protection rituals and spells have one thing in common: they're done outdoors, with the land. It makes sense to include the land spirits in these workings, as they're already present for them.

There are three components to truly inviting the land spirits into your workings, as you've seen throughout the exercises in this chapter:

- Adding an invocation of the land spirits to your wards, witch bottles, and other protective spells
- Incorporating materials from the land itself in the workings
- Being mindful of the ways these practices affect the land spirits

These are all necessary steps on your path of inviting the sacred wild to work with you in sacred reciprocity. Protection is in the best interests of all spirits on your land, human and land spirits alike. As guardians of land themselves, the land spirits are truly your greatest allies for protection magic.

Ritual: WARDING YOUR HOME WITH THE LAND SPIRITS

Whether you move to a new home or you simply haven't done a protection ward yet, this is a great ritual for long-term protection in your home. You'll be inviting the land spirits to help you in creating this ward and providing the ingredients. I recommend having everyone who lives in the home present for this ritual, if possible. You will also need to know the cardinal directions as they relate to your home before you do this spell, as you will be addressing each direction.

Materials Needed

Trowel or shovel

Personal effects from members of the home or of members of the home who will participate in the ritual (one thing per person)

4 stones (collected during the ritual)
Offering for the land spirits

Directions

1. Go outside to your land spirits altar or place of connection. Ground and center.
2. Pour out or place your offering on your altar. Ask the land spirits to guide you toward four rocks to use for warding your home and land.
3. Walk around your property or neighborhood until you have collected four stones. If you are doing this with others in your family, have each person collect a stone. This is an intuitive exercise in and of itself, as you are finding the stones you feel called to.
4. Return with the stones to your altar. In the following steps, you will call in each element, starting in the east, turning to each direction and lifting a stone up to the sky as you invoke the elementals. If there are other people present with you, they can invoke an element if they feel called to, or you can do every element.
5. Turn to the east, holding up the stone, and say, "Guardians of the East, Element of Air, creatures of wing and sky, I invite your blessings of new beginnings to our home. May only opportunities of abundance and kindness find us here, and may all negativity be stopped at your border. Hail and welcome." Place the stone on the altar in the eastern direction.
6. Turn to the south, holding up the stone, and say, "Guardians of the South, Element of Fire, creatures of heat and poison, I invite your blessings of desire and passion. May only opportunities of excitement and joy find us here, and may all negativity be stopped at your border. Hail and welcome." Place the stone on the altar in the southern direction.
7. Turn to the west, holding up the stone, and say, "Guardians of the West, Element of Water, creatures of sea and river, lake and

ocean, I invite your blessings of loving relationships and the flow of natural emotions. May only opportunities of respect and honor find us here, and may all negativity be stopped at your border. Hail and welcome." Place the stone on the altar in the western direction.

8. Turn to the north, holding up the stone, and say, "Guardians of the North, Element of our Mother Earth, creatures of wood and field, I invite your blessings of stability and grounding to our home. May only opportunities that help us build on our solid foundations of protection and love find us here, and may all negativity be stopped at your border. Hail and welcome." Place the stone on the altar in the northern direction.
9. Stand facing your altar and say, "Spirits of this land, I invite your blessings to this home. May my home, my family [names of all members of the household, animals included], and myself [your name] be blessed, protected, and safe from harsh weather and extreme dangers. May no one enter this boundary of protection except those who bring warmth, welcome, and love. May it be so."
10. Have everyone present touch each stone and breathe onto it to imbue it with their energy.
11. Bury the stone for air and personal effects for each family member in the easternmost part of your property, saying, "Guardians of the eastern land, winds of Euros's warmth, land spirits of the air, and all spirits present here this day, I invite you to join me in protecting this land, this home, and the loved ones therein. May no one enter this boundary of protection except those who bring warmth, welcome, and love. May it be so."
12. Bury the stone for fire and personal effects for each family member in the southernmost part of your property, saying, "Guardians of the southern land, winds of Notos's nurturing rains, land spirits of fire, and all spirits present here this day, I invite you to join me in protecting this land, this home, and the loved ones

therein. May no one enter this boundary of protection except those who bring warmth, welcome, and love. May it be so."

13. Bury the stone for water and personal effects for each family member in the westernmost part of your property, saying, "Guardians of the western land, winds of Zephyrus that bring fertility to this land, land spirits of water, and all spirits present here this day, I invite you to join me in protecting this land, this home, and the loved ones therein. May no one enter this boundary of protection except those who bring warmth, welcome, and love. May it be so."
14. Bury the stone for earth and personal effects for each family member in the northernmost part of your property, saying, "Guardians of the northern land, winds of Boreas that bring storms of change to this land, land spirits of Earth herself, and all spirits present here this day, I invite you to join me in protecting this land, this home, and the loved ones therein. May no one enter this boundary of protection except those who bring warmth, welcome, and love. May it be so."
15. Once you've buried each stone, you can optionally return to the center of your land for meditation on connection and protection with the land spirits.

These wards will stay active indefinitely. If you move, you can dig up the stones, but it's not necessary, because you used stones from the land itself. If you find you need more protective energy or something has shifted, cleanse and clear the energy of yourself and your home before repeating this warding practice.

CHAPTER 5

Weather Magic

Weather magic is a powerful practice to engage in with the land spirits. Much of weather magic is tied to tuning in to the water cycle, which is another expression of the cyclical nature of life. This is the wisdom of the sacred wild, to live by the cycles of nature, and weather is a key part of that.

You can use weather magic to direct action to encourage weather of a specific type, like a rain dance, or it can be about building a relationship with weather spirits. Weather magic can be complicated or simple. Whenever we hope for a snow day from school or that rain will hold off for an event, we are practicing weather magic. Through communion and observance, such as trying weather augury or learning weather lore, we can gain knowledge of the weather spirits and start to understand them.

As with the best of all magics, weather magic is not about blatant control for the sake of feeling powerful, although there is something truly empowering about being able to affect the weather. Often we use weather magic to ask for rain to subside while we wait at the bus stop or for a storm to bypass us so that flights won't be delayed. We might even invite rain to help our crops or combat wildfire risk in early summer, or we might invite sunshine for a friend's wedding day. But you don't always have to actively do spells or rituals to engage in weather magic. Observance and understanding are a clearer way forward to working in harmony with nature. Whenever we are in harmony with nature, this is magic in and of itself.

Weather Spirits Among Us

Recognizing the spirits in the weather around you is an example of animism. An animistic understanding of weather is more present in our modern world than you might expect.

In modern Greek, the words for north and south are still *boreas* and *notos*. The word for sea is still *thalassa* (θάλασσα), a goddess who personified the sea in ancient times. The rivers are still named for the gods whose dominion they were. The word for a full moon is still *panselina* (πανσέληνα) referring to the goddess of the moon, Selene, and her lover, Pan.[28]

English-speaking cultures do this process of animistic naming as well. Often, we name weather spirits without calling it such. Each hurricane is given a name, personifying it for many reasons. One, it makes it easier to talk about, plain and simple. But two, it helps the threat and danger feel more approachable. I'm not going to say you can stop a hurricane with your force of will, but we can connect to its energy.

I've never worked with hurricane energy personally, as I've never lived close to a hurricane zone. But I have appealed to weather spirits to help during a wildfire surge in Greece in 2023. Rather than asking for rain, which would be out of season in the heat of summer and actually detrimental, we appealed to the land spirits to calm the fire spirits. It seemed to help, as the megafires—a new category of threat to wildfires in the past few years—ceased that week.[29] The more the climate changes, the more the chance of extreme weather does too, and being able to call upon weather spirits and land spirits will be increasingly necessary.

It's not a coincidence that people are being called to work with land spirits more and more in this time of tumultuous weather. It's the spirits of the four winds and the land itself meeting and inviting our spirits to join the conversation. As the need for protection of the land increases, so must our relationship to these protective spirits. The land and weather spirits

---

28. Lucian of Samosata, *Dialogues of the Gods*, in *The Works of Lucian of Samosata*, vol. 1, trans. H. W. Fowler and F. G. Fowler (Clarendon Press, 1905; electronic reproduction by Sacred Texts Archive), sec. 6, https://sacred-texts.com/cla/luc/wl1/wl113.htm.

29. Elyse Welles, "Living in Greece and Wildfires," The Wild Hunt, July 31, 2023, https://wildhunt.org/2023/07/living-in-greece-and-wildfires.html.

are not who we need protection from; we can seek protection by working together with them.

What Are Weather Spirits?

In the tradition I teach, the Sacred Wild, as well as in my training with the Faery Tradition, weather spirits are seen as an extension of elementals. Winds bring air elementals, earthquakes awaken earth elementals, storms bring air and water elementals together, and so on. We will look at named examples later in this section, but the difference between elementals and land spirits is mobility. Weather spirits, by their very nature, are impermanent in any one place. But they are still intimately connected to land spirits work because the land can sense the coming changes and work with us to prepare or divert weather.

There's a dance of connection when a weather spirit enters the area of effect of a land spirit. The land starts to prepare for the coming weather spirits, sometimes months in advance. And if they haven't prepared, the land will simply not welcome that weather. This might look like the leaves falling off the trees faster than usual in the autumn when warm temperatures come unexpectedly, as I witnessed in October 2024 when we experienced a drought. It might sound like emissaries chattering among themselves—crows gathering in trees, squirrels meeting on extended branches. Trees may seem to close in toward each other, as if huddling before the winds pick up. And when good weather is coming, it's like the emissaries and guardians know before anyone else, as they seem to reach toward the expanding sunlight.

I've seen land spirits deflect weather. Often this is simply to protect a small area, and you probably have heard of this too. A house completely missed by a tornado. A falling tree that, despite what the laws of physics would predict, missed whatever was in its path completely. These are examples of how weather spirits can act of their own accord with protection in mind, and having a land spirit as your first line of defense against these big forces of energy is the key to success.

I have a theory that the people who found themselves saved by the weather's sudden change of pace or strength in their immediate vicinity had a right relationship with the land. Not necessarily in an intentional land spirits practice, but words are only so good at describing reality. Maybe these people garden ethically, have recently helped a wild animal cross the street, resist raking their leaves, feed the birds in their yard, get vet care for the stray cats in their area, or some other good deed that has endeared the land spirits to them. And the deeper we make that relationship with the land through our work with land spirits, the more protected we'll be in natural storms.

There are certain types of weather that feel more enspirited than others. Rare weather events like ball lightning or the finding of fulgurites (lightning-struck earth) feels magical for its uniqueness. Fog is a liminal form of weather, making it a potent time to meet the weather spirits and even invite them to be a conduit for magic. In Debra Burris's iconic book *Weather Magic*, she writes a meditation to connect with ancestors during fog because of its ability to "open foggy channels of communication."[30]

If you witness special events of weather, consider its meaning for yourself. Pay extra attention to signs and ideas that come to you during this time. As a rule, I've found extreme or unexpected weather to be a sign of change coming either in my own life or in society—local, national, or global.

Sympathetic magic, the idea that the qualities of the weather reflect the needs of the spell or working we are doing, is an important part of weather magic. Collect storm waters to harness their power for use in spellwork for anger or protection (we will discuss storm waters later in the chapter), or use cold weather to aid in freezer spells or similar emotionally cold bindings or magical workings. When you need confidence or are doing any work on your solar plexus, sunny days are an aid to this work. The weather around us affects us more than we often realize, and weather magic gives us an opportunity to tap into that effect and make use of it with intention.

---

30. Debra Burris, *Weather Magic: Witchery, Science, Lore* (Llewellyn Publications, 2024), 105.

Exercise: COLD WEATHER FREEZER SPELL

Call on the weather spirits next time you need to conduct a freezer spell. Freezer spells are ways to stop people or situations in their tracks. They aren't permanent like bindings or banishings but are more of a way to take a break. Freezer spells do not send harm to the other person, although the effects of what happens when you stop their interactions with you is something to be aware of and consider.

This is a spell done only when the temperature is below freezing. The point is for this to freeze in the elements, aided by the land and weather spirits.

Materials Needed

Uncoated paper
Pencil (not pen)
Silicone or plastic mold that you can freeze
Tablespoon of water (or enough to submerge the paper in the mold)

Directions

1. Take these spell ingredients outside to where you can leave them, at least overnight to freeze.
2. On a piece of paper, write the person's name. If it's not the whole person you want to stop interactions with, but a situation or a certain subject you want to avoid, write this instead.
3. Place the paper at the bottom of the mold you'll be using and pour the water over the top. Say, "As this water is to this paper, may [thing you wrote on the paper] freeze in their tracks. May it be so."
4. Place the container where it will freeze. In the morning, remove the item from the mold, then leave the item where it can naturally decompose when it melts.

As this will eventually melt, you may need to do another freezer spell indoors in your freezer if the person or situation begins to bother you again. Or you may reevaluate and do another working like a binding or banishing instead. The purpose of this spell is to give you time and space to decide what to do.

Wind Spirits

Some weather spirits have names, also indicating a deeper, long-held truth of them as omens or harbingers of certain types of weather. For example, the idea that the north wind brings bigger storms is true in most places I've visited and lived, in the UK, the US, and the Mediterranean.[31] There's science behind that as well, but the personification of the North Wind as an elemental power is a widely applicable ancestral folk connection. The North Wind is a character in Aesop's Fables, tales attributed to an ancient Greek slave and storyteller.[32] The tales date to between 620 and 560 BCE, but these timeless stories have become part of the fabric of Western cultural understanding of land spirits as well.

In ancient Greece, the North Wind was called Boreas. All directions of wind had names as well. They were collectively called the Anemoi and were seen as representatives of certain types of weather and seasons.[33] The Romans had their own equivalent names for the four winds, or the Venti, as they called them. Keep in mind these are the seasons of the Mediterranean, so the roles of the four winds might apply differently in your part of the world, but they are mobile, so I would consider them present wherever you are.

---

31. George MacDonald, *At the Back of the North Wind* (London: Strahan & Co., 1871), 63.
32. Aesop, *Aesop's Fables* (Guizhou Renming Publisher, 2009), 64.
33. Luke Roman and Monica Roman, *Encyclopedia of Greek and Roman Mythology* (Facts On File, 2010), 14.

Direction	Greek Name (Anemoi)	Roman Name (Venti)	Season & Weather
North	Boreas	Boreas	Winter. Cold weather and storms.
East	Euros (pronounced *EV-rohs*)	Eurus (pronounced *YOUR-uhs*)	Autumn. Warm, sunny days. (Autumn is a second growing season, not a time of decay in Greece and Rome.)
South	Notos	Auster	Late summer to early autumn. Brings warm, calm, nurturing rains.
West	Zephyros	Favonius	Spring. Brings fertility to the land by carrying pollen to cause fruiting and blooms.

Exercise: ANEMOSCOPY—WIND DIVINATION

This exercise allows you to use the wind to indicate the favorability of a certain situation or course of action.

Materials Needed

Ribbon

Stick strong enough but not too thick to easily be stuck into the ground

Compass or a compass app

Correspondences chart of the Anemoi (Greek four winds) found above

Preparation

Tie the ribbon to the stick and place the stick in the ground so that the ribbon can blow in the wind.

Directions

Set your intention, taking your time to form it into a question. When the wind is calm, ask your question aloud. On the next gust, see which direction the ribbon blows. Look at the correspondences of the Anemoi and see what this suggests about your situation. You can read this most clearly in a yes or no fashion, similar to a pendulum. If the ribbon blows west or south, it is favorable. If north or east, it is a bad idea.

Storm Waters

Waters collected from storms are a powerful way of inviting the land and weather into your magic. Different types of waters have different magical uses. Here's a brief guide to the type of water you can collect and what to use it for. Always be safe when collecting water. Leaving containers secured outdoors while you are safely indoors is always the best option. I also recommend straining waters collected before storing to remove any organic materials that might cause them to spoil.

Stump Water

Stump water is my favorite water to use in workings. Stump water is the water found in stumps or hollows of trees after a heavy storm. I love that this retains not only the power of the storm but also the grounding energy of the earth that received that rain. I use this water in workings for healing, grounding, and calming spells to relieve anxiety or worry surrounding a situation.

Snow and Snowmelt

Snowmelt is the water left over from melting snow. Collecting snow to be used in magic at the moment is powerful, but just because it's melted doesn't mean it's lost any of its magic. Use snow or snowmelt in magic to cool down a situation: to stop it from escalating, and to cool the tempers of those involved.

Hail

Frozen ice particles that fall like rain, hail is dangerous but powerful to use in magic. Always wait until the hail has passed to go collect hailstones, and wear proper head and eye coverings. They can be used in workings to be tough on a situation or to bring tough love into a relationship where it's needed. It's also useful for dissolving barriers when used in sympathetic magic to emulate a hard situation dissolving as the hailstone melts.

Exercise: HAILSTONE SPELL FOR FORGIVENESS

Use hail when you need to dissolve pressure or animosity between people.

Materials Needed

¼ cup salt, or enough to cover the plate or bowl
High-lipped plate or a bowl
Hailstones for each person

Directions

1. In salt next to each other on the plate or bowl, write the initials of two or more people who need to forgive and move on from their tensions and animosity.
2. Place a hailstone on each person's initials.
3. Let the ice melt, relieving the tension and showing that these two people can get along just as their initials and hailstones can blend into one.
4. Dispose of the salt and water mixture in the drain, as salt water can kill plants. As it flows down the drain, feel the tensions dissipate and leave for good.

Sun-Shower Water

Sun-shower water is water collected during a brief rain that happens while the sun is still shining. It is extra potent if collected while the sun and a rainbow are visited. Use this water in gratitude workings: sun-shower water reminds us that even when things are gloomy, there is hope. Sprinkling some over yourself when you are in need of a boost of positivity is a great way to use sun-shower water.

Thunderstorm Water

Collected during a storm (the bigger the better), thunderstorm water is powerful for resolving or placing hexes, curses, bindings, banishings, or baneful magic onto others. It basically adds a punch of power to your magic. Use it to dress candles or sprinkle it onto a cord before doing a cord cutting for added oomph. It also is powerful for binding bad habits for yourself. Never go outside during a thunderstorm. Before a storm comes in, leave buckets outside to collect the water for you. Only collect your water once the storm has safely cleared.

Exercise: BINDING BAD HABITS WITH THUNDERSTORM WATER

When you have a habit you know you want to kick, this is a working to try.

Materials Needed

Firesafe twine
½ cup thunderstorm water (enough to soak firesafe twine in overnight)
2 bowls
Black candle

Timing

Most workings I've shared have no specific timing required, but as this one is about setting new intentions and banishing old habits, doing this on the dark moon (the day the new moon is completely invisible) is a powerful addition to your working.

Directions

1. On the night of the new moon, often called the dark moon, soak the twine in thunderstorm water in one of the bowls. Take the candle and dress it in thunderstorm water as well. As you do so, imagine the habit you want to end dissolving in your life. See yourself not doing it—what are you doing instead? If it will be saving you money to quit this habit, how will you spend your newfound prosperity? Focus on the way you're changed by this habit leaving you.
2. Leave this overnight, outdoors on your land spirits altar if possible, where it can bask under the darkness of the new moon.
3. The next morning, take the twine out and hang it up where it can dry. Set the thunderstorm water aside for the evening when you finish the spell.
4. That night, go back out to your land spirits altar and wrap the candle in the twine. Focus on the habit being bound by this twine as you wrap. Feel the habit's power over you fade.
5. In the second bowl, melt a bit of the candle's bottom and stick it to the center of the bowl. Pour the thunderstorm water into it, leaving a small layer of water at the base of the candle.
6. Light the candle, and as it burns down, scry into the flames and the reflection of them in the water for signs. These signs may give you an indication of what ending this habit will be like, the challenges you might face, and how to overcome them.
7. Meditate as the candle burns down, and when it fizzles out in the water, pour the ashes and remains at the base of your land spirits altar. You can bury the wax remains with the water, digging a small hole at the base of your land spirits altar, or set them aside to be burned with loose incense and a charcoal disk. Don't wait on this, though. Do it now or the next morning.

This working is repeatable for other habits, but always one at a time. If the habit comes back, the working can also be repeated to reassert the habit's binding.

Hurricane Water

Use hurricane water for baneful workings but also to channel anger and rage in clear ways. It is also very powerful for clearings. Simply sprinkling hurricane water in the corners of your home will cleanse any negative energy.

Never go outside during a hurricane. Placing buckets to collect hurricane water before it comes through is the only safe way to collect it.

Exercise: ENERGY CLEARING WITH STORM OR HURRICANE WATER

This can be done with either thunderstorm water or, for a really powerful clearing, hurricane water.

Materials Needed

Plant wand: Use any plant you feel it is permissible to cut a small branch from, but I recommend pine, eucalyptus, lavender, rosemary, or sage. You will need 1–5 branches about 8 inches in length. Make sure they're not too wide to feel comfortable in your hand together.

Bowl of storm water (you will need at least ¼ cup)

Preparation

You do not need to wrap or tie the plant wand. Simply hold the bundle of herbs in your hand. You will use this to flick the water out in the rooms of your home.

Directions

1. Open all the windows in your home and the doors if possible.
2. Invite the spirit of the storm to come in safely on the wind, saying, "Cleansing wind and clearing rain, with your powers come again. May all energy stagnant and stuck be removed from this place, leaving a clean slate of healthy, energizing, positive air in this home."

3. Walk through each room of your home, going into each corner and flicking the water with your plant wand to clear the home. Repeat "Cleansing wind and clearing rain, with your powers come again" as you move through your home.
4. When you are finished, offer this water to the land spirits at your outdoor altar or at the base of a tree.

This working can be repeated anytime the energy feels stale or stagnant in your home or if a bad experience happens there.

Weather Augury

The land is the first to know about incoming weather patterns. Your relationship with land spirits leads you to have a deeper, quicker understanding of weather changes and storms to come by encouraging listening to the land for its signs that changes are coming. Reading these signs is a form of augury. Weather augury is the skill of knowing how to read the signs from nature to understand impending weather. To augur means to predict what is to come, and so we learn to see predictions in weather and nature that we might not otherwise notice.[34] The word itself comes from an ancient practice of seership used in the Roman government to predict the future when making important decisions.[35]

Exercise: NEPHELOMANCY—CLOUD DIVINATION

Nephelomancy is an ancient form of divination using the observation of clouds.[36]

Materials Needed

Cloudy day and a safe location to lie on your back and observe clouds
Your land spirits journal
Writing utensil

34. *Oxford English Dictionary*, "augury (n.), sense 5," last modified June 2024, https://www.oed.com/dictionary/augury_n.
35. *Oxford English Dictionary*, "augury (n.), sense 5."
36. Anonymous, *The Encyclopedia of Occult Sciences* (Robert M. McBride & Co., 1939), 267.

Directions

While lying on your back, observe the clouds. If there is a specific message you're hoping to receive or an element of your life you need guidance on, ask the clouds to help you see clearly the advice nature has for you. You can trace them into your journal, or just list the shapes and things you see within the clouds. These are some things to look for:

- Shapes that look like people you know
- Body parts and their symbolism. For example, a nose could mean staying sharp in a situation, or eyes could mean you need to look deeper into things.
- Numbers, either directly (e.g., the shape of a number nine) or in numbers shown to you as a repeating sequence of clouds in particular numbers (three small clouds in a row, for example)
- Animals and their meaning, either personally or traditionally
- The way things connect into each other as the shapes change. For example, when a cloud starts out by looking like a fox and then morphs into a dragon shape, it may be symbolizing how you need to shift your perspective from being cunning and reactive to being in control of the situation.

This is not an exhaustive list of things you may see, but it should give you context and ideas for other observations you may have. Repeating this exercise regularly for guidance will improve your observation of the signs and help you build a log of what means what to you.

Weather Lore

Weather lore includes cultural sayings that ask us to look for certain signs to understand the weather ahead. Weather magic isn't always about what we're manifesting; it's sometimes about what we're observing. This is what weather augury, and understanding our regional weather lore, is all about: observing the signs so that we can live in greater harmony and preparation for what's ahead.

Land spirits can work with nature to send active signs to you about the impending weather. When you step outside in the morning on your way to work, you might be tipped off by a wind picking up just as you consider grabbing your gloves or not, guiding you to bring them. You can even directly ask the land spirits about the impending weather and see what response you get. A murder of crows blocking out the sun as they fly overhead as you ask if there'll be clouds today would be a very auspicious indication of yes. Asking if it'll get cold enough to need a jacket just as a delightfully crunchy leaf falls before you is another clear sign: bring the jacket.

Weather auguries are sometimes personal. But there's also established augurs that people look for to know what kind of weather is expected, and these are what I call examples of weather lore. You also might employ knowledge of numerology when counting passing flocks of birds or if you notice a particular shape in the way a cloud is formed. The possibilities of where to see signs in the sky are endless. This is also where weather lore comes in to provide clues.

In North America, I was always taught that if the maple leaves are showing their undersides, then a rainstorm is coming. My Amish babysitter used to say that if the animals are grouping together, a storm is coming. These are ways the land spirits communicate with those who are willing to look around and notice the signs.

Here is some other North American folklore of weather indications that I have observed as messages from the land spirits:

- When I was growing up, it was always said that when the first wooly bear caterpillars show up, there are six weeks until winter. Some say that the width of the red stripe in the middle indicates how long winter will be, but I've charted that loosely since I was about seven years old and haven't found that to be overly accurate.
- My mom always said that if your houseplants start to curl their leaves under, the first frost is nigh.

- Groundhogs and their shadows featured heavily in my Pennsylvania upbringing, although the town of Punxsutawney was a few hours away. Groundhog Day is February 2, and a designated groundhog endearingly named Punxsutawney Phil will come out of his house and look at the ground. If he sees his shadow, there will be six more weeks of winter. If not, spring is coming fast. While this isn't always true in my own observations, I did notice that once the groundhogs start to appear regularly above ground, there will be no more frosts.

Weather lore is a fun and varying practice with traditions across the world. The fun part for me is looking for those synchronicities. Those are often the folkways that prove true. Taking note of these, looking for ways they manifest to similar or different effects—for example, maybe animals huddling doesn't bring rain where you live but it does bring high winds—is a great way to connect to the weather spirits by starting to understand them.

Exercise: LOCAL WEATHER LORE

What are the signs and symbols of certain types of weather where you live? Ask the older folks in your life or those who have lived where you live longer than you. Check the weather forecast and start to look for signs that might be indicative of if it's correct or not—if they said rain is coming, did you see animals huddled? Record your observations and then take a look over the coming months to see if the folklore is true.

The Responsibility of Weather Magic

Ethics are personal, but they're important to consider when engaging in weather magic. When you engage in weather magic, you are accountable for whatever happens. Weather magic is far-reaching, so the people, animals, and events affected by your magic may be hard to predict before the damage is done. Does this uncertainty affect the way you engage in weather magic? Many people aim to harm none in their magical practice.

How does weather magic factor into your moral code? For these reasons, consider carefully before practicing weather workings.

Do some reflection in your land spirits journal. What are your ethical considerations regarding using weather magic? Where would you feel comfortable using magic to change the weather, if ever? What about augury or other techniques to connect with weather? Record your thoughts in your land spirits journal, and as you engage in weather magic, come back to this entry and reevaluate. As with all beliefs and ethics, yours may shift over time, and this is a normal part of spiritual growth.

Looking for ways weather magic is truly beneficial is a complicated process. Rain dances are found in cultures across the world because rain is the key to life.[37] It's life-giving water gifted from the atmosphere to us. But knowing the atmosphere and needs of your land are important. Rain is often beneficial to our land, but heavy flash flooding is not. If I were to call in heavy rains in wildfire season, I'd cause destruction of potentially greater quantities than the fire would have wrought due to mudslides. This exact phenomenon happened in 2023. Red-alert thunderstorms raged from September 25 through 29, 2023, across Greece. Hundreds of people were evacuated due to mudslides caused by unexpected, early storms, and this spread across the Peloponnese on the mainland and out into the islands as well.[38] My family was part of the rescue efforts to help the animals of the Peloponnese be evacuated from shelters. Although the country was still burning from a summer of wildfires, these rains were certainly not an improvement for flora or fauna. Working with the land spirits to appeal to the coming rains, for instance, and invite their rain but at a slower, gentler pace is a good idea.

When we are working with weather spirits, we're joining an existing harmony with the land spirits and weather spirits, not seeking control. See weather magic as an opportunity to open a dialogue, and see your work

37. "Rain Dance," *International Feminist Journal of Politics* 9, no. 4 (2007): 558–59, doi:10.1080/14616740701608307.

38. "Echo Flash: September 25–29, 2023," European Commission, Emergency Response Coordination Centre, https://erccportal.jrc.ec.europa.eu/ECHO-Products/Echo-Flash#/echo-flash-items/25747.

with weather as a collaboration led by the land spirits as the experts on what is needed. The following meditation invites you to be a part of this collaboration of weather and land.

Meditation: MEET THE WEATHER SPIRITS

This meditation is best performed outdoors before an impending storm. Be responsible, however: never go outside when there is a risk of lightning. Go outside before the storm arrives. If you feel safer, or if the storm is moving in quicker than you expected, do this meditation indoors while it is coming in. Once you've mastered the connection in difficult weather, the coming of good or more subtle weather is possible too.

This isn't a traditional meditation, more of a focusing exercise. Storm energy is powerful for magic of all kinds. Doing this as the start of a ritual for change—a working to remove someone from your life, a spell to protect your home, a spell jar to quit smoking, an oath to commit to healthier boundaries, and the like—is a great idea. Weather magic is a wide and varying practice that can complement any spellwork you're doing, but begin with a foundation of protection based on building simple connection. Your land spirits will back you up.

To begin, go outside and stand somewhere you can open your arms comfortably. Under a porch is fine if the weather is already picking up, but somewhere you're directly in contact with the earth is best.

First, plant your feet. Focus on the way your heel is pressing on the ground. Focus on the sole and ball of your foot. And finally, focus on the toes themselves. Wiggle them: each toe is connecting you to the earth, solidly. You are grounded here. You are anchored and connected to this earth in this moment. Call the land spirits to you, and let them know verbally or by thinking it through and letting the emotions of that situation flow through you into the ground.

Place your hands at your sides, palms out, as if feeling for an energetic shield before you. Breathe in and out through your nose, focusing on the smells you can identify. Do you smell rain? This is usually the smell of soil mixed with a gentle, slightly metallic scent. Can you smell the leaves? In autumn, the leaves of a storm smell distinctly different from the almost tropical green scent of a summer rain. What is the wind bringing with it? Do you smell manure from the farms down the road or the fragrance of apple blossoms? Is there snow or sleet in that wind?

Start moving your hands up and around in the air around you, slowly feeling the pulse of the energy of the storm. Allow yourself to connect with its energy, visualizing or sensing the slight electricity in the air connecting to your palms and traveling through your arms, the solidity of the ground traveling up through your feet and into your legs.

Feel this energy meet in your sacral chakra, grounding you in the land for this moment. Allow this grounded, electric energy to fill your chest as you continue inhaling the weather of the present moment. Now allow it to move up through your heart and your throat and settle behind your third eye. As it flows to your crown chakra, feel it flow outside you. The energy of the storm flows through you and out of you through your crown.

Feel the warm, tingling sensation at the top of your head, feel the winds whipping against your skin, feel the cold in your fingertips, feel the barometric pressure in your legs as you stand tall. It might feel uncomfortable at moments, but remember you are safe, held in the bosom of your land spirits. Focus on the connection you're building, the fullness in your experience of this coming storm.

Now, you are fully connected and immersed in this storm. If you'd like to, at this point you can request protection from the coming weather, verbally or internally. Say, "I ask that my family [state names] be protected in this coming storm," or "May the storm blow over by [a certain time or event]."

When you're ready, let your connection to the storm flow out of you in the reverse way you connected. Close your connection from your crown chakra. Inhale the land around you and exhale the connection to the storm with each breath—feel the flow move down through your chakras, out through your arms, and finally through your feet and into the earth again. The last thing you should feel is the land spirits still with you. This isn't a problem—smile and send love as your last energetic exchange before going back inside for a warm cup of tea.

CHAPTER 6

Plant Allies

The land spirits *are* the environment. As I covered in chapter 1, they're not metaphors and they're not personifications of natural phenomena. They are real, animistic presences on the land. But they are also part of an egregore: the environment around you. Plant allies, including trees, make up a lot of the energies you will feel in a natural landscape. In this chapter, I'll cover how to connect with plant allies, their connection to land spirits, and how this will deepen your work with the land.

Your Plant Allies

Similar to the wards I discussed in chapter 4, you can also work with plant spirits to create protective boundaries, cleanse, or otherwise curate the energy of your space. Plant spirits are individual spirits shared by plants of the same species. Individual plants have their own temperaments too. The longer a plant knows you, the better you'll get to know it. But the overarching species of a plant has common attributes, properties, and likes and dislikes. Much like a dog has both breed-specific qualities and personality qualities, plants are unique but reliably researchable.

The right plants for your situation will serve as guardians of your land, joining the land spirits in their shared interest of protection, but also affecting the overall feel of your land. A poison garden, for instance, has a very different feel from a culinary one; a hedge of blackberry bushes is different from a hedge of honeysuckle or jasmine. Every grove of trees has a different feeling because of the types of trees there, as well as the lichen, moss, fungi, or other ground cover you might find nearby. The plant spirits of a given area create a symbiosis that contributes to the egregore of your land. This overall energetic imprint will have an effect on you or others that might come across your space.

Working with plant spirits might bring to mind images of plant healing or gardening, but you can work with plant allies without ever owning a trowel or pouring a tincture. You do not have to be a gardener or herbalist to have a relationship with plant spirits. Start by acknowledging and identifying the spirits of the plants already growing around you, especially the weeds you might overlook. If you don't have land of your own, there's still something growing somewhere nearby.

Even if it's just stubborn sidewalk dandelions or scraggly city-planted trees, these are enspirited allies in your neighborhood. Get to know these plant spirits, introduce yourself to them, and research their properties. Identify the plants in your area. Choose the most common plants around you, perhaps the ones you notice the most in your time outside, and research their properties and components. Dandelion, for example, is very activating for the solar plexus chakra. It aids in digestion and helps you know how to best express yourself. Does that message resonate with your life? Record in your land spirits journal the plants you are drawn to and their properties.

Bringing Plant Allies into Your Life

While planting plants, flowers, trees, or other plant allies is one option, there are plenty of ways to connect to plant allies wherever you live. If you are a city dweller or have limited control in the plants around your home, a houseplant or even a dried branch or wreath is a means of inviting these plant spirits. If you do live somewhere with a garden or nature nearby, you can connect to those spirits by bringing them inside. You can add some of these elements—such as leaves, acorns, twigs, feathers, eggshells, or anything you find that feels safe to remove from nature—to your land spirits altar or simply anywhere in your home. One of my favorite ways to bring plant allies into my home is by making a seasonal wreath each year for protection.

Exercise: PLANT ALLIES WREATH

No matter where you live or how in the broom closet you need to stay, a wreath is a socially acceptable decoration to have in your home. Wreaths are traditional blessings used by cultures across the world. In India, garlands of mango leaves are hung at the front door to invite prosperity, and lemons and other citrus are hung to ward away negative energy.[39] In many European cultures, evergreen boughs were brought indoors as a symbol of long life to ward away winter ills. In Celtic cultures, the evergreen is particularly spiritual as a symbol for vitality and immortality.[40]

Materials Needed

3 feet of length for a base plant to form the wreath's foundational, circular shape (see following tips)
5 to 10 flowers or plant materia
Other decorative elements or charms (optional)
Firesafe twine or wire
Nail or over-the-door wreath hanger

Tips for Choosing a Base

You can buy a wooden or foam frame that can be redecorated for each season with fresh ingredients, or make a new one when you want to each year. For natural bases, evergreen forms the basis of many wreaths, especially in winter when the energy of vitality is important. But there are many other plants you can use as well. Any thorny, spiky plants are protective. Nettle should be rinsed thoroughly to remove its stinging properties, and gloves would be wise for handling roses and brambleberry varieties like blackberry, raspberry, or huckleberry. All of these would form a beautiful base for a

---

39. "The Symbolism of Mango Leaves in Indian Tradition and Culture," *Atulya Events* (blog), April 8, 2024, https://atulyaevents.com/the-symbolism-of-mango-leaves-in-indian-tradition-and-culture/.

40. Eliseo Mauas Pinto, *Celtic Tree Wisdom and Magick* (pub. by author, 2013), 27.

wreath. Using lavender or jasmine is a great way to invite the energy of self-love and self-care. And any plant ally you enjoy spending time with is a great foundation for your wreath. You could even take a fallen branch from beneath the willow tree in the park.

Tips for Choosing Other Plants

Once you have your base picked out, you can add other intentional elements you want to call into your home:

- Lavender to promote calm and self-love
- Eucalyptus to encourage focus
- Dried orange or lemon slices to remove negative energy and protect from curses and the evil eye
- Succulents for strength

Optional Elements to Include

You can even add charms or talismans like an evil eye, the Italian horn, a *glücksschwein* (good luck pig), an om symbol, or other symbols that speak to you and your journey.

Directions

Take the 3 feet of your base plant and twist into a circle. Use your twine to tie it every 3 inches so that it will keep its form. Once your base feels secure, you can begin tying the flowers to it. With each new addition, thank the plant spirits for coming into your home and lending their power to your life. Remind yourself why you chose what you chose: thank the lavender for bringing calm, ask the nettle to bring you protection.

In my tradition and many others, saving old wreaths all year and burning them at a sacred balefire at Samhain, the Witch's New Year, is customary, but this is not necessary. Returning them to the earth by burying or composting is just as well. This is why I specify firesafe twine: if you used any materials that are not biodegradable or firesafe, discard in your normal garbage.

Plant Allies Wreath

Trees as Guardians

Land spirits and plant spirits work harmoniously on the land. If there were a family tree of related energies, it would be clear that plant spirits are more closely related to land spirits than any other kind because they grow in the earth, becoming part of that earth as they pull in nutrients from soil. While rivers and rocks are part of the land, trees essentially are created of the land. Land and plants stick together in an understandable relatability of stability to one another. For this reason, plants are often guardians, particularly trees.

When you looked around for a guardian of your property, chances are good that you discovered it to be a tree. Trees carry such a deep, rooted connection to the land spirits. As guardians, they are connected to the power of the elder land spirits themselves. The old trees on a mountain carry the energy of that mountain, just like the stalagmites and stalactites of a cave are the energy of that cave.

Trees are such powerful spiritual conduits of energy that they have their own mythology, such as you might find in Celtic and Greek cultures. In Ireland, the ogham, an alphabet of medieval Ireland, has been purported to represent specific trees and hold power as sigils representing the power of the trees.[41] In Greece, dryads are specific spirits of different types of trees, and hamadryads are the spirits of a specific tree at a given location.[42] These are by no means the only ancient cultures with trees sacred to them. Banyan trees are sacred in India, and I saw many altars placed under them in villages throughout my visit in Greece. And Yggdrasil, the famous Norse Tree of Knowledge, is another ancient cultural example. This shows an ancient understanding of trees as twofold plant spirits: both of their species and as an individual.

Researching the mythology of your guardian is a great way to connect more strongly with them, especially if this is where you have built your land spirits altar. This research, as the ancient examples show us, should include an understanding of the species' lore in a global way, as well as any individual lore you can find for the area you're in. For example, if you live in Kentucky and your guardian is an oak tree, you might research the Celtic associations of Oak, while also looking up Appalachian folktales about oak trees and asking the human elders of your community—visiting historical societies can be helpful here too.

Trees also have a strong connection with the fae. From modern tales, as found in the television show *Stranger Things*; to marketing tools, such as the Keebler Elves; to the ancient talk of fairy portals in trees, it is a common motif that trees hold the gateway to fae and the spirit world.[43]

To be clear, trees are not the only plant allies that serve as guardians. Other plants with long histories in the area can also be guardians. Weeds like dandelion and hardy brush and scrub plants are often too strong to be totally removed by even the most aggressive human actions, and they also

41. Charles Graves and C. Limerick, "The Ogham Alphabet," *Hermathena* 2, no. 4 (1876): 443, https://www.jstor.org/stable/23036451.

42. Jennifer Larson, *Greek Nymphs: Myth, Cult, Lore* (Oxford, 2001), 11.

43. Weronika Łaszkiewicz, "Into the Wild Woods: On the Significance of Trees and Forests in Fantasy Fiction," *Mythlore* 36, no. 1 (2017): 47, https://www.jstor.org/stable/26809256.

tend to be overlooked as just a part of the scenery in woodlands and the borders of farmland. Anyone who has ever tried to uproot dandelions knows that their roots grow wide, long, and strong—they are very deeply connected to the land on which they grow. Brush plants, especially those that extend across a large area, can be guardians, for their far-reaching effects.

Mycelial networks are how the mushrooms of a place are all connected to each other. They might be the most powerful spirits of place to work with because, as studies continue to show, they are connected with the land deeper than any plants.[44] Mushrooms are so tied to the land that they can even be elders themselves: the oldest being on the planet is a mushroom that extends three square miles across Oregon's Blue Mountains. This is both the oldest and largest living organism on Earth, known as a honey fungus (*Armillaria*). This "humongous fungus" has been around for at least 2,500 years.[45]

The guardians of a place are so much more prevalent than we first think. With this new information on plant allies, go outside and look for more guardians. Is there a hedge near your home? What is it made of? Is there ivy or other extensive, far-reaching plants you can identify? Record your findings in your land spirits journal.

Exercise: BONDING WITH MUSHROOMS

Next time you find yourself near wild mushrooms growing outdoors, practice this bonding exercise. Mushrooms are guardians that connect deeply with the land—what we see above the ground is only the barest hint of their extended, underground mycelial networks. In this meditation, seek to connect to them at their source.

All you need is a place where mushrooms are actively growing. Sit down, if able, with your palms down on the ground near where they are growing. Never touch mushrooms found outside,

---

44. Mohammad Bahram, and Tarquin Netherway, "Fungi as Mediators Linking Organisms and Ecosystems," *FEMS Microbiology Reviews* 46, no. 2 (2022): fuab058, doi:10.1093/femsre/fuab058.

45. Jason Daley, "This Humongous Fungus Is as Massive as Three Blue Whales," *Smithsonian Magazine*, October 15, 2018, https://www.smithsonianmag.com/smart-news/mushroom-massive-three-blue-whales-180970549/.

as they may be poisonous or toxic and touching them could transport the spores, so be sure you are a safe distance from the growing mushrooms.

When you are seated comfortably, with your hands on the ground if able, close your eyes. Ground yourself and bring your attention to your palms against the ground. Do you feel the warmth of the earth beneath your palms? Visualize the mushrooms rooting deep into the soil.

See the way the little spores showing themselves at the surface are connected to their roots. See, in your mind's eye, how those roots continue deeper and deeper, wider and wider. Imagine what that grid can look like, all unseen beneath you.

Now, see if you can feel the pulse of that connection in your palms. Feel for that warmth beneath the surface of the ground, and let it pulse into your palms and up through your arms. This connection to the mycelial network reminds you that you are part of the ecosystem of nature too: your roots of connection to the earth are just as unseen as those mycelial networks are on the surface.

Let this circulation of flow between the mushrooms and your energy continue as long as you are comfortable. When you feel this connection start to fade, send gratitude down your palms and out to the mushrooms for connecting with you today.

Repeat this exercise at other mushroom locations and with different species. Record in your land spirits journal each time you do, so you can begin to notice similarities or differences in different mushrooms.

Working with Land Spirits Through Plant Allies

Working with plant allies is a way to connect more deeply to the land spirits. There are plenty of books on tincturing, essential oils, extracts, infusions, balms, salves, teas, tisanes, powders, poultices, and flower essences—even taking supplements in capsule form is a way to invite the energy of a plant into your body. You'll find many in my recommended reading section at the end of this book. These are all viable ways to connect with a plant and to heal, grow, and work through shadow work. We'll talk a bit more specifically about flower essences in the meditation at the end of the chapter, but for more specific workings with plant allies, specifically from a professional herbalists' perspective, many, many authors have got it covered.

You do not have to be an herbalist to work with plant allies. My favorite way of working with them is to connect with the plants directly where they grow. Be mindful when harvesting plants that you do not remove more than 10 percent of their growth. This is my own measure. And never cut them back to the roots. If you do have to harvest a root, do so with deep reverence. Leave offerings and thank the plant profusely. Honor them in your work with that root and know the power of what you hold in your hand.

This path of land spirits work is about connecting on the level of plants and land: that means recognizing their autonomy and right to life. Of course, as gardeners know, gardens are a brutal world of death and competition. But when we engage with plant allies, especially those in their own environments and wild places, it's best to do so in flow with their needs as much as possible.

Finding the ways you best enjoy working with plant spirits is the journey of magic, in many ways. With regard to plant allies in their relationship to land spirits, there are some plants you should get to know more than others. It's not the prettiest flowers or the most expensive oils that make the biggest difference in our connection to the land. Often, it's actually the "ugly," unnoticed plants we need to work with. Making a tincture of bramble or a nettle tea from your own land or neighborhood is more powerful than store-bought essential oils, in my opinion, and meditating with that bramble beforehand is a great idea too.

When working with plant allies, remember that it is about building sacred relationship, and sacred relationship is about reciprocity. What we give to the plants is what we can expect in return. If you spray your yard to kill dandelions, you will not have a good relationship with dandelions! Be aware of the ways your choices and actions on your land affect the relationship you can have with the spirits who live there.

Meditation: FLOWER ESSENCES WITH PLANT SPIRITS

This meditation invites you to connect with the plant spirit while making a flower essence. While flower essences were popularized in the early twentieth century by Dr. Edward Bach, this meditation and my own work with flower essences are inspired by the work of Nicholas Pearson in his book *Flower Essences from the Witch's Garden*, a book I highly recommend for further study and research into flower essences and their properties.[46]

Note that you can also make this exercise part of a wider ritual of connection to plant allies, but I do recommend approaching the plant alone so you can connect more fully and personally to its spirit.

Preparation

You will need a sterilized bottle or jar to collect the water. Any glass jar or bottle can be sterilized by placing it on the stovetop in a saucepan, boiling water in a kettle, and pouring the water over and into the jar. Let it rest until cooled, then dry it with a clean towel. Alternatively, you can buy a brand new bottle or jar that is already sterilized.

Materials Needed

Bowl filled with 6 ounces of water. Tap is fine but distilled is even better because you want to diminish as much as possible what organisms or bacteria could grow in your water. To achieve a result similar to distilled water, you can also boil it and then allow it to cool. Never make flower essences with hot water, as it could kill the plant.

Cheesecloth or light towel wide enough to cover the bowl

Camp chair and blanket (optional)

---

46. Nicholas Pearson, *Flower Essences from the Witch's Garden: Plant Spirits in Magickal Herbalism* (Destiny Books, 2022).

Sterilized bottle (at least 6 ounces) to place the essence in
Brandy or another consumable preservative, like citric acid
Mesh strainer

Directions

1. Once you have your ingredients, take your bowl filled with 6 ounces of water, along with the cheese cloth or light towel, to the plant you want to communicate with. You will be placing the branch or flower of the plant in the water for several hours, allowing its essence or imprint to be left on the water. As the term suggests, flowers are the best means of essence-making, but if the plant you're looking to connect to doesn't flower, a lively branch will do.

   Note: Ideally, you won't have to pick a flower to rest it in the bowl of water—if there's a way to position the bowl safely in a way that allows the branch or flower to rest in the bowl, that's great. If you do have to pick a flower, please be aware of foraging guidelines in your area and if it is safe to do so. If there is a risk of overharvesting, do not pick the flower. If it is something like a dandelion, clover flower, dead nettle, or another plant that is often killed as part of lawn maintenance, picking one of these flowers is unlikely to cause environmental harm. Always use your best judgment and the research available to make an informed decision regarding environmental concerns.
2. Once the flower or branch is in the bowl, cover it with the cheesecloth or towel to keep bugs and other impurities out. This pure flower essence you'll be creating today is called a mother tincture, and you can dilute it further and further into lower dosages for magical uses. Diluting is especially recommended for poisonous plants. I recommend consulting Pearson's book for more on uses and dilutions.
3. Find a place you can sit or lie down next to the plant. Bring a camp chair or blanket if you wish. Ask the plant to gift some of

its energy to you into the water. Explain what you'll do with it. Use your intuition to feel if the plant is amicable to these terms, and answer any questions you feel it might have—who you are, what your needs are, and why. Even if the plant isn't listening or following what you're saying as such, you're clarifying your own reason for being there, and that's great. When you feel an intuitive acceptance of what you're doing, readjust yourself to be comfortable on the ground.

4. Put one hand on the ground, and the other on the plant, if able. Close your eyes. Feel yourself seated on the ground. What parts of your body are touching the earth? Feel yourself solidly on the ground beneath you. Now focus on your hand on the plant—the pulse of energy there that is the spirit of the plant. Imagine its roots beneath the ground, how they twist and flow out into the soil around you. You are seated above its root system too, just like the flower or branch you're creating an essence from.
5. Now imagine that plant's roots coming up from the ground, beneath your body, and grasping you in a warm embrace. Flowing up and over your legs, pulling you closer to the earth, snugly. You are connected to this plant now, physically and spiritually. Feel those roots extend upward, branching around your torso in a gentle embrace. Feel the thin vines caress your arms, surrounding you up to your collarbone like an ornate necklace. Little leaves emerge, maybe even flowers too, as the plant extends to your crown chakra, creating a literal crown softly resting atop your head. You feel the front of these soft branches against your third eye, and the properties of this plant flood through you. Protection, prosperity, calm, focus, or energy, whatever this plant is known for, you're feeling its effect. You know that when you're ready to leave its embrace, the essence of this connection will stay with you in the mother tincture you created.
6. While the essence will need 3 hours to be properly infused into the water, you can meditate with the plant spirit only as long as

you need to. When your essence is complete, strain it into your sterilized bottle and add a few drops of brandy or your preservative. This mother tincture can then be diluted further for dosages, and should be stored in a temperate, dark environment for up to a year.

CHAPTER 7

Urban Land Spirit Work

Working with land spirits in cities is just as powerful as working with them in nature. While a connection to and a respect for the natural world is necessary for land spirit work, having an abundance of untouched nature around you is not. In fact, you might find land spirits have a greater need for connection with you in spaces with less natural beauty.

As foreign as land spirits are to humans, imagine their perspective. They began their existence with the earth itself in a time when there were no people; they've seen so much change, growth, loss, and decay in the span of their existence. To imagine the world as they first came to it—or even as they've largely experienced it, in a humanless capacity—is beyond our fathoming.

In some ways, for them to imagine the world as we see it is also difficult. Think of how complicated and confusing the modern world must be to land spirits. Their gentle, residual energy is quickly treaded on by the human energies of war, social division, protest, politics, economic hardship, social change, fashion, technology, and more. Combine that with the rapid industrialization, even by human standards, of the past two hundred years, and the difficulty in connecting with land spirits in cities begins to make a lot of sense. They've been quickly—and in some cities, thoroughly—usurped and disregarded.

When you first reach out to the spirits of the land itself in a city, the first perception you'll receive won't be a land spirit at all. The egregore is infinitely more perceptible and dominant in cities. As I explained in chapter 1, the egregore is the layers of energy that create the overall feeling of a place. The egregore is more present in cities than land spirits are for two reasons. First, there are way more humans than nature found in a city, so the human-made energies of an egregore will simply override any subtler, natural energies. Second, the land spirits don't really want to be on the surface of cities, so the egregore forms a sort of shield against the trauma they've experienced. By being the first layer of defense, it gives the land spirits permission to hide beneath it.

I teach and was taught that time and energy are the two components that compose reality. How we spend those two resources, as well, determines our experience on this earth. Land spirits experience time extremely differently. The only way we can connect is with energy. And when they've gone millennia—which to them might feel like the blink of an eye—in which humans have suddenly stopped connecting to the earth as much and indeed are causing destruction and change at rapid rates, the land spirits are certain to be distressed or at least wary of what is happening. The land spirits that inhabit cities feel this distress all the greater.

In places like rural India, rural Greece, or even Middle America, the land spirits might reside on the surface. In untouched landscapes and undeveloped mountaintops, the land spirits are more present than any other kind of spirit. But in cities, you have to dig beneath the human-made egregore and the trauma shield surrounding the land spirits to connect with them.

Let's play devil's advocate. You don't live on the land directly, so what's the point of connecting to the land spirits when you live in a city? In your land spirits journal, record all your fears and concerns about working with land spirits in the city. As you grow in your connection to land spirits in your city, review these concerns and see if you have alleviated them. This will empower your land spirits practice.

Discovering the Egregore

Modern, everyday humans living in the city create the egregore in everything they do. This often leads to a phenomenon in which the egregore itself invites a certain type of human to want to visit or live there. People move to New York City to get inspired by music, art, architecture, acting, dancing, and so many other creative arts, that the egregore itself quickly becomes one of creativity. Los Angeles too attracts fame-seekers and go-getters, ageless beautiful people, and those comfortable with a public persona, and so this egregore is loud and competitive, but also tinged with beauty and creativity. In Athens, most Greeks move there for education, and the overtone of the egregore is one of history, academia, and the light, fun spirit of colleges.

It quickly becomes a question of the chicken and the egg: Was it the egregore that beckoned a certain type of person to know they'll fit in there, or do people create the egregore they need? The answer is probably both. Connecting with the egregore often simply means going out and being within it, and letting it affect or guide you in some way—trying new things, dancing when you usually would stay seated, talking to new people. Sometimes the most spiritual work we do is in a public place surrounded by strangers doing something very mundane. Living in a city is very much like that.

Echoes of the Past

There are other spirits beyond living humans and historical events that make up an egregore. The dead are roaming the cities more than any stereotypical haunted farmhouse—in fact, I have a theory that we notice spirits in rural homes more because there are fewer general spirits. Cities have more people, which means more dead. And many people who live in a city might live their whole lives there. Not only that, more so than folks living in rural areas, people walk around and interact with the city itself. They leave a residual energy behind if they've walked a certain route over and over again for many years on their way to work, school, or home. And often spirits will haunt these exact routes, intentionally or unintentionally.

Battlefields, execution grounds, prisons, and individual places where people died in distress often harbor spirits of the dead more strongly than any other places. Cities have locations where folks were held up at gunpoint, robbed, or worse—that contributes to the gloomy, heavy feeling of egregores in some parts of cities more than others. This contributes to the general egregore too, even as those individual spirits might still inhabit those spaces.

Interestingly, this close connection to the veil seems to draw the living much more than deter us. Los Angeles, New York City, New Orleans, Gettysburg, the Somme, and Normandy are all famous locations for pilgrimages and desired destinations for folks to visit or live in. This is another testament to the power of the egregore, that it draws us to the lessons of human experience, good and bad.

Exercise: GETTING TO KNOW THE EGREGORE OF THE CITY

Write down as many adjectives as you can think of to describe the vibe of your city. Ask other people who live there how they would describe it. What do they say? Is there any commonality? These will be the energies of the egregore that you can reach beneath to connect to in the next exercise.

Working with the Egregore

The egregore in cities is dominated by human actions and emotions. All the good and the bad that we go through as a collective are exacerbated by cities: lots of people living in close proximity leads to heightened, more perceptible collective change. As witches, pagans, and spiritual practitioners, we're often at the forefront of political change. We have to be, as members of marginalized religious groups. If we're not defending the rights of marginalized communities, including BIPOC, LGBTQ+, women, and above all, intersectional folks, we're not living up to the charge placed on us as dwellers at the crossroads.

Working with the egregore might look and feel harder than working with land spirits alone. That's because it's more related to our journey as humans in this life. Egregore work often has us confronting base truths of the human condition and our place in the world. Whether you believe in incarnation or are simply an animist, consider how you feel about the purpose behind your magic. Are we here to effect change for other humans or simply to continue our own soul journey of growth? Is the earth more important than individual human life? Equal? Reversed? And if so, is that reflected in your magic? Before consulting the egregore for magic, knowing these deep levels to the intention of what you're doing is important.

It's also important to remember that when seeking connection to the land spirits in a city, you're not working against the egregore. You're seeking to understand it, feel it, and then begin to reach beyond and below it to find the land spirits in their quiet refuge beneath the shield of the egregore. The egregore protects the land spirits from the first effects of human emotions. This was a hard concept for me to grasp at first.

The first time I tried to connect with land spirits in an urban environment was a Baltimore Reclaiming ritual. We met indoors in the center of the city and conducted a ritual of planning. We would be invoking the spirits of the city to help us plan the coming Wheel of the Year. We were on the top story of an old factory that had been converted to meeting rooms and shops.

The session began with the leader of our circle talking us through a grounding exercise. She asked us to reach down with our spiritual roots and connect to the earth and the spirits here. She told us to see these roots growing down, past the piping of the building and continuing through the floors beneath us. I tried, imagining them stifled and stiff under the asphalt street. I tried to reach out to the spirits of the land of Baltimore.

But I remember thinking, "There's something else in the way." I couldn't visualize it strong enough: the roots I envisioned coming down through myself and into the ground just weren't penetrating. Even when I sensed the energy of the land spirits, it wasn't my impression that they were interested in joining us. In fact, they didn't seem interested in even acknowledging our spiritual call.

We were sent straight to spiritual voicemail.

I was dismayed and confused, but excited to try again somewhere else on my own later. I finally met the land spirits of Baltimore, but it was in the cemeteries and church graveyards, the liminal spaces of crossroads and the harbor. But why wouldn't they answer when I was downtown? I've since wondered if it was because of the spirits of the once-factory or if the energy of the crowded, confusing buildings of many offices with various purposes threw off their ability to connect directly with us. I've also wondered if I just wasn't spiritually strong enough to connect; maybe land spirits of cities are just too hard to reach. But what I've realized is that the barrier of connection I felt was the egregore: the collective energies of all that Baltimore has been and still is. And I had to connect with them first.

Simply acknowledging something and working with something are two different things. Even if I'd called it out as the egregore at the time, I don't know if that would've been enough. It's the intentional connection that matters, the directing of my energy toward it, with purpose.

Exercise: BEING PART OF THE CITY'S EGREGORE

This exercise asks you to tap in consciously to the egregore and your place in it. If you connect with the energy of the egregore on its own, you'll know what it feels like. Then when you seek the land spirits and feel something else, you'll be more confident in knowing it was the land spirits you felt.

Materials Needed

Your land spirits journal

Preparation

Go somewhere you won't be disturbed directly but where you are part of the action in your city. This could be a public park, the library, your favorite diner, a bench near a crosswalk, or even your own apartment balcony if there's lots of city to observe from there.

Directions

1. Sit or stand, whatever is more comfortable. Do not close your eyes for this, even though it feels meditative. Look around at the energy of the city happening around you.

2. Breathe deeply and long, really feeling the breath enter and leave your lungs. On your inhales, feel the way that you are pulling the egregore within yourself.
3. On your exhales, understand that the breath you release is your offering to the egregore: it is how you are part of the ecosystem of energy.
4. As you breathe mindfully, look around at what is happening around you. Notice the people and how they interact with each other. If you're near any trees or plants, do the people notice them? Are there dogs enjoying the land? What is the feeling of watching these people—does it feel busy, do they feel disconnected from one another, or is there a cohesiveness? Do you feel anyone's emotions? Sadness, loneliness, happiness? You might feel that some or many of the people have a wall up around themselves, like they're shielding themselves from being a part of the community as much as possible. Notice this.
5. As you observe these emotions and events flowing around you, focus on breathing that in. As you're breathing in, think about the egregore entering your body. You are a part of this. What color is the egregore? The first color that comes to mind is the dominant one. Other colors may start to punctuate your mind as well.
6. See the colors flow into you with each inhale. How does the egregore feel as you breathe in? Is it warm and caressing as it enters your body through your breath? Is it cold and calloused? Do you feel any emotions that you didn't feel at the start of this exercise start to rise in you? You might be picking up on these emotions you noticed in others.
7. As you exhale, focus on what you want to contribute to the egregore. How do you want to be felt by it? How does your energy fit in or oppose the energy of those around you? Is there a color you're releasing into the egregore? You are a part of the tapestry,

a color on the palette, an important dot in the matrix of the city. Allow yourself to feel that.

8. Record your experiences in your land spirits journal before leaving this place so the experiences are fresh.
9. When you're ready to disconnect from the egregore, ground and center and raise a shield. This allows you to return to your own energy and release the energy of the city.

You might feel tired or overwhelmed after this exercise, so get a snack and take time to relax and reset.

Locational Balance

Looking to understand the egregore is the first step to starting to connect to land spirits. Beyond the spiritual connection to the egregore we can do, we also must start at the mundane, surface level: researching the history of the land. The individuals and families who built the town, the locations of violent events, the politics and unrest, the biggest achievements and accomplishments—looking at these facts helps us make connections between the feelings and overriding impressions of a place. If a history has been mostly positive, the land will feel more inviting and uplifting to live on and vice versa.

I call this locational balance. Similar to the way we view personal balance, the locational balance is the points for and against reverence and respect for nature, including human nature and free will, that a place has experienced. If you are in a place with heavy oppression of a marginalized group, and the history of that place is one of slavery followed by segregation, with considerable relocation and harm to the native populations to boot, the locational balance will not be good. Humans have wrought more destruction on our planet than any other species in nature's history.[47] But this is exactly why we need to do egregore and land spirits work.

---

47. Damian Carrington, "Humans Just 0.01% of All Life but Have Destroyed 83% of Wild Mammals—Study," *The Guardian*, May 21, 2018, https://www.theguardian.com/environment/2018/may/21/human-race-just-001-of-all-life-but-has-destroyed-over-80-of-wild-mammals-study.

Those of us who are awake to these sufferings are the ones who can help alleviate them. The land is suffering because of human actions, and humans are suffering due to other humans too. We are the humans who are here to heal ourselves, the collective, and of course, the land. The egregore holds much of the energy that needs to be healed in humanity so that we can work to heal the land. Whenever we work to heal and transmute pain experienced in the egregore, we are helping the land; when we work with the land, we are helping the egregore. These concepts are tightly intertwined to create the environment of a place.

Lessons not learned in the past are destined to be repeated in new ways until they are. I've seen this on the East Coast of the US—in places that will remain nameless for reasons you can guess at the end of this example. The individual Native American tribes resisted uniting against the colonizers, which ultimately led to their demise. Similarly, in these counties today, locals who are part of organizations and clubs—from local business leagues or even book clubs—have trouble working together to enact change and growth for the community as a whole. The lesson that needs to be learned is the importance of coming together, and these rifts will likely continue until at least one community group, or one generation of that community group, decides to stand up together and build unity.

Cities are the site of massive energy exchanges, such as protests, parades, and historic events. The spirit of those events lingers on in the egregore, so if a city has passed a certain law that led the majority of citizens to feel a certain way, that will compound into it as well. Unrest or unhappiness carries stronger than joy, but I've been in cities where things are going extremely well, and those places have a strong feeling of those good things too. It's an extrapolation of the same effect that happens in a single household. If folks have been fighting, the energy is noticeably different from when everything's going well or if someone just told a joke. Egregores are that energy on a massive scale.

Exercise: THE MYTHOS OF THE CITY

What are the myths of the land you're in, if any? Any cryptids known to walk this area? Any urban legends? Even if you think the answer is no, google it and see what you can find. Add to these thoughts with your own myth of your city, or create the outline of one by answering the following questions: If you could tell a story about the land, what would it say? Who would the main characters be—buildings, landmarks, figures in history? How would you personify the egregore? Record your creative expressions in your land spirits journal, or make a collage that represents this mythos. Giving a visual and allowing yourself to express the character of the city is the key here.

Reaching the Land Spirits

As I've said, land spirits are more easily accessible in places with nature. While land spirits are found beneath every apartment complex and shopping mall, they're easier to access in places with less distraction. Cemeteries and church graveyards, parks and green spaces, and the liminal spaces of crossroads, riversides, and harbors were the main places I was able to connect to land spirits when I lived in Baltimore. If you're looking for land spirits in any city, these are the places I would recommend you search.

Once you've engaged with the egregore and done your best to understand a bit about the energy of your city—the politics, the local communities of pagans, witches, spiritual practitioners, and otherwise—you're ready to meet the land spirits. If you've lived in your city a while, you might have already met the egregore too; this process isn't yearslong but continual as you engage with the city you live in. Reaching beneath it to the land spirits is a matter of knowing where the shield ends. Separating egregore from land spirit is a mental spiritual exercise that might take some time.

Land spirits in cities versus rural places are like Hurons versus Ents. In *the Lord of the Rings*, Ents are sentient tree-like creatures that pre-date the other species of Middle-earth substantially.[48] They are the perfect example of a nurtured, empowered guardian of the land. But what about the other sentient trees in cities, on battlefields, or worse, that have been destroyed or desecrated by humans and other species? These are Hurons. They're

48. J. R. R. Tolkien, *The Two Towers* (HarperCollins, 2004), 89.

also sentient, but they've learned to harden their heart, keep quiet, and not engage with the outside world. Some of them barely seem alive anymore, they've been so downtrodden by the world around them. Hurons are much more likely in cities.

When you reach out to work with Huron-esque land spirits, you might be the first altruistic person they've met in a long time. Be patient and continue trying even if you're feeling like they're sending you straight to spiritual voicemail like they did to me the first time. Going to the greenest, largest spaces in the city, like London's Hyde Park, New York's Central Park, or the central cemeteries are great places to meet them (cemeteries have fewer humans in them than you might expect). I also recommend going just outside the city limits and working your way in over time. In Philadelphia, I felt the land spirits as I rounded the Schuylkill River right off Kelly Drive; in Baltimore, they loved the Inner Harbor and Fort McHenry.

Exercise: REACHING OUT TO LAND SPIRITS IN URBAN PLACES

As time goes by and you reach out to the land spirits of your city more and more, you can feel them more easily in populated places. But to reach out for the first time, I recommend going somewhere more accessible like those places shared previously.

Materials Needed

Offering (I recommend your hair if you live in that city)

Preparation

Go to a place as natural as possible while still being in the boundaries of your city, such as those listed in the previous section (parks, graveyards, etc.).

Directions

1. Recall the egregore connection exercise (see page 120). Drawing in the colors of the egregore, remind yourself of what it feels

like to connect to the egregore. Breathe in the egregore, exhaling your connection to the city. See that breath as offering.

2. Now, ground and center. Feel your feet solid on the earth. Breathe in the colors of the egregore again, and this time let that flow down through your body and into the earth. Feel the flow of the egregore into the land and the way that seeps out and around you into the city itself.
3. While accepting that that flow is happening, detach yourself from it. Recognize that it is happening around you. When you're detached, draw your attention to the land itself. It should feel like an earthy green color, deeper, thicker, and somehow quieter than the egregore. If you are a less visual person, focus on the solidity of the ground beneath you. The grass, the dirt. The trees, the quietness compared to other places in the city. This is the land spirits' domain: simple, earthy connection.
4. When you feel the land, release your offering. Hold out your palms to the ground, and send love and connection out of your hands and into the earth. Introduce yourself. Send your apology for what has happened on the land; allow the land to feel your ardent, honest grief, and most importantly, the love that grounds that grief. Remind yourself and the land that it is the love of land that allows you to feel so connected to its suffering. You are in this together.
5. See your color, your energy, flowing out of your palms and feet and into the land.
6. Feel the land receive your energy. Let the land spirits flow up into your palms and through your feet.
7. Feel this flow of warm green energy, a circuit of love and connection. Remind yourself of the egregore's flowing colors, tapping back into that flow. Feel the difference between them both. And begin to recognize their cohesion.

You are a part of this flow of egregore and land. Tap back into these energy flows anytime you call on the land in your work, repeating this as needed.

Offerings for Urban Land Spirits

Leaving offerings and spending time in those places will warm up the land spirits to work with you in the city proper as well. Some of the best offerings, I've found, are those of service. Cleaning up litter, removing graffiti, safely and ethically cleaning headstones, or simply spending time watching and listening for what those land spirits need goes a very long way.

I also found singing to be well received. There's a whimsy to the land spirits in cities that might catch you off guard. I get the impression that some of those land spirits have grown and been affected positively by the large human influence on the land, and those are always fun to encounter! New Orleans's jazz clubs, Budapest's Szimpla Kert (in the Jewish Quarter), and Munich's English Garden all stand out to me as places where the spirits of place are present and happy to be there. But by and large, be patient with the land spirits in cities.

Because these land spirits have been neglected for so long, it's important to resist asking for anything in return right away. It might take some time for these spirits of place to warm up to you. The slogan of Baltimore is unofficially "You'll get used to it." I found that to be the case for land spirits as well; they just have to get used to you. Once they do though, they're just as responsive, helpful, and valuable as allies for your spirit team, and maybe more so, as they'll deeply appreciate your efforts.

Exercise: MAKING AN URBAN LAND SPIRITS ALTAR

Altars are wonderful places to leave offerings. Building an urban land spirits altar to your city is an offering on its own, but it's also a place to leave offerings to your local land spirits privately. Find some iconic items that really stand for your city. Keychains with mascots, postcards for tourists, wrappers for iconic candies, coffee cups from famous coffee shops, menus from iconic restaurants, candles made by a local business, and so on.

Make an altar for the city itself, and start to connect to the egregore more intentionally. This will enable you to feel the egregore and thereby separate it out in your own energy from the land spirits. And as you grow in connection to your local land spirits, place the gifts they give you on this altar too. This altar will be a visual, physical reminder of the energy flow that they are both a part of—and that you're a part of too. If any of your family grew up in this city, put their pictures on this altar if you feel called to, in the spirit of this deep connection.

Be an Ambassador for the Land Spirits in Cities

Local events, from good news to tragedies, will mold the ever-changing egregore. Staying involved and aware of those things will give you a clearer path forward to connecting with the land spirits because you'll be able to discern what's what. You're also showing your interest and connection to the land. You have a unique opportunity as a person who is in touch with these spirits to be an ambassador for the land spirits. You can stand up for them, protecting green spaces with your votes and showing up to planning committees and local meetings with their interest in mind. You can join protests or volunteer for community works. And if there's a Reclaiming group in your area, I can't recommend their good work enough. Founded by Starhawk and others in the 1970s as a fusion of the Goddess movement and political activism, today the focus of the group is the Fivefold Agenda, focusing on equity, diversity, and "sacred values" of "peace, community, [and] family" for progressive social, political, environmental and economic activism.[49] Most Reclaiming groups have open events for you to join without committing to a full coven structure, so they're perfect public rituals to whet your feet in the local witchy community. Chapter

49. Starhawk, "About—Five-Point Agenda," Reclaiming Collective, accessed November 25, 2024, https://reclaimingcollective.wordpress.com/about-five-point-agenda/.

11 focuses strongly on how you can work in partnership with the land no matter where you are.

Meditation: BENEATH THE EGREGORE: CONNECTING WITH URBAN LAND SPIRITS

In the dark of the night, in the quiet of the morning, in the bustle of the midday, and in the waning light of sunset, the city goes through immeasurable changes and flows every single day. It's a miracle machine, really—all the moving parts that come together to bring function to the city, from the trash crews to the linemen to the city workers and police departments. It's an overwhelming amount of people to simply keep the ship afloat. This energy of symbiosis is what we'll try to tap into today.

Find yourself seated and comfortable somewhere you can hear all the noises of the city. Outdoors is best, or open a window. Note the time of day too, and consider what might be different at other times of day (repeating this exercise at other points of the day is a great way to get acclimated to the environment as well). Bring a journal with you to write any noticings or revelations at the end.

Once you're comfortable, close your eyes. Breathe gently and steadily and open your ears to the city sounds. Try to match the sounds to their purposes and origins. Are there any sounds you can't recognize? How far out do you think you can hear right now? Now start observing with your nose. What are the smells—yes, even the bad ones! Identify what you can and see if you can match any of the sounds to the smells. Are there other smells you can't identify? Note those sounds and smells and open your eyes. What can you see that matches the sounds and scents you've experienced? What can you see that you can't hear?

Now it's time to feel. How do you feel about all that is around you? How is it making you feel? Remember that these are two different things. We can feel a certain way because of our own associations with something, such as the sound of construction happening across the street making you feel annoyed because you had an ex who did construction work. And we can also be made to feel something by the sensations the source is actually causing, such as tension at the vibration of a jackhammer or cold at the feel of the wind moving past you.

How do you feel about the city? What is the energy of this city, in your experience of being here? Imagine taking that energy and experience and condensing it, balling it up, gathering it all together. Picture it lifting off the ground, away from your ears and hands and body, and forming a cloud above you. What's underneath? What is the energy beneath that now-removed energy? Those are the land spirits. Reach out and leave them an offering. Ask them how you can best reach them and care for them. Introduce yourself and state your intentions of connection. When you're ready, release the cloud, and open your eyes. You should still be able to feel the presence of the land spirits. Write down what it feels like, and practice tapping into them regularly.

CHAPTER 8
Sacred Places

What makes a place more sacred than another? What designates a sacred site, like Stonehenge, Varanasi and the Ganges river, or an ancient Greek temple? Is it the human consecration element, or is it the inherent presence of the land spirits? In this chapter I'll share how the combination of these factors has us surrounded by sacred places, and how we can connect with them.

My business, Seeking Numina, began as a personal quest to connect to sacred sites and the spirits found there. *Numina* means "a spiritual force or influence often identified with a natural object, phenomenon, or place" and comes from Latin.[50] Living on three continents, I've spent most of my life visiting sacred sites, from the big ones to the unknown ones and everything in between.

Sacred sites are usually places of human-assigned significance and are often connected to a deity or well-known spiritual experience. In a way, a sacred site is an egregore, not just a place. It is a layered, unique place for human activities that is usually said to have inherent divine qualities. Visiting sacred sites gives us the chance to explore new, powerful energies and tap into them for healing and spiritual nourishment. Often it is a chance for pilgrimage, such as to the temples of deities one might work with or to a cultural landmark one might have associations with and connections to.

50. *Merriam-Webster Dictionary*, "numina," accessed November 25, 2024, https://www.merriam-webster.com/dictionary/numina.

These connections are a spiritual calling to a particular place, instigated by a spiritual experience, or by seeking ancestral connection.

Defining a Sacred Place

A sacred place can be anywhere that has a particularly powerful energy that you can connect with and experience in a unique way at that location alone. These aren't always recognized as such by any authority. The Standing Stones at Avebury, Machu Picchu, or the Holy Sepulchre of Jerusalem are sacred places widely known. But you might find a certain grove on a certain trail near your house has something special to its energy. Something you can't quite touch. These are sometimes called portals, but I find that takes some of the earthiness out of it. It's not an otherworldly experience to be in a truly sacred place: it's very much of and with this Earth, our mother, and all her beauty. They are certainly portals to connect to the land spirits that make that place so special.

Our ancestors saw sacred places as the site of collective and personal healing, often in communal activities, such as the celebration of the Eleusinian Mysteries at Eleusis or the Arkteia dance at the Temple of Artemis in Vravrona. At holy wells like St. Brigid's Well in County Clare, Ireland, personal healing could be sought. At the Oracle Chamber in Malta, remembrance of the ancestors was the main purpose. But the thing all sacred sites have in common is their ability to allow visitors to connect more deeply with the spiritual world within and around us.

Exercise: SACRED PLACES VISION BOARD

This exercise allows you to create a visual representation of sacred places that matter most to you.

Materials Needed

2 pieces of paper
Pen or pencil
At least 5 images of sacred places that will fit on a piece of paper (I recommend printing these out from the internet.)
Glue stick

Directions

1. On the first piece of paper, create a mind map for the definition of sacred places. Write "sacred places" in the center and then circle it. Surround this central word with the words that stand out for you about sacred places. What do they feel like? What qualifies them as such in your estimation? Do any places stand out to you right away that you want to write down? What goals would a sacred site have, in your definition? Start tuning in to these qualities. By building vocabulary and understanding around sacred places, you are creating a framework for your experience of sacred places. You'll be able to tune in to places that fit this feeling more easily. Tip: building a framework for sacred places works best if you meditate on and sit with these feelings often.
2. Create your vision board using what inspired you from this exercise. What are some sacred sites you've always wanted to visit? Find images of these places, or draw them yourself. The discovery of these places is a fun part of this journey too, if no places come to mind. Cut out and glue the pictures onto your second piece of paper. You can hang this vision board above your altar, or place it in your land spirits journal.

Finding Sacred Places

Sacred places can be found anywhere. They can be human-made, or they can be natural sites. They're found in cities and middle-of-nowhere places as well. When you find one, you'll have a few factors to tip you off.

- They feel out of time and space. Sacred places are places that have unknown depths to their energies. You'll feel the sensation of time slowing down. This sensation might be more apparent when you leave and compare and contrast your feelings at the site and after.
- These are places where land spirits and other spirits of place feel accessible. You might feel watched or like you walked in on something. When you reach out to the spirits of place at sacred sites,

they are more powerful and therefore more tangible for your six senses (the meditation on page 146 is a great starting point to connect at sacred places).

- You feel healed. Mental and spiritual healing is the main purpose of temple sites and established sacred sites. If you're intentionally connecting to a sacred place, such as hanging a clootie at the entrance to a sacred well in Ireland, leaving an offering, performing acts of service, or simply doing some deep breathing and observance in a grove you come upon on a hike, you'll feel these benefits.

These are the main things that separate a sacred place from an ordinary one. Although moments of healing or sacred connection can happen anywhere, when it feels outside of yourself, there's something inherent in the land spirits there that is contributing to it.

That doesn't mean sacred sites have all been found and cataloged, however.

Some of the most powerful sacred sites you'll come across when you start to look might not have labels, names, or reputations at all, and that makes them all the more special.

These places are usually tied to liminality. If there's a collective of trees near your house with just enough room for you to cast a circle in between them, don't be surprised if you feel a surge of welcoming energy. Crossroads are spiritually powerful as well, so much so that Hekate is the goddess of these spaces in Greek mythology and in conjunction with modern witchcraft. Where the sea meets the shore, where the river meets the mountain, behind waterfalls, and inside caves are other liminal places where you can meet powerful land spirits, making these sacred sites. Often, temples are built at these liminal places, such as the Temple of Hera in the Corinthian Gulf or the Temple of Poseidon at Cape Sounio. Down the road from the temple of Liminal Hera in Perachora, I found a cave that has no known spiritual history, but when I set foot inside, there was no denying the powerful spirits of the place.

Some sacred places are simply healing and empowering to behold, and further research might guide you to learn there's more significance to that place than you expected. Chickies Rock is a place I pilgrimage to every time I visit Pennsylvania, my home state in the United States. As far as I know, it's not on anyone else's radar as a sacred place; it's not in any guidebooks or online blogs for Lancaster as such. Even our known history of the Native American relationship to the land at this place isn't conclusive on its significance, though we do know that the name, Chickies Rock, comes from the Chiquesalunga Creek, meaning "Place of the Craw-fish."[51]

Interestingly, when I tell folks of the spiritual power of Chickies Rock, they often agree with me. So I set out to uncover a bit about the history and geology of the place. The ridge that forms Chickies Rock is itself a liminal space, as it is an outcropping overlooking the river. It is also made entirely of quartzite, a well-known spiritual conductor.[52] And historically, there were three witches who lived in a home at the peak.

In the early 1890s, the trolley company of Lancaster County wanted to purchase their home to build an amusement park and new tracks on its site. When they refused to sell, they were forced out by the company's granted eminent domain. Forced out of their home, they cursed the land and the town around it. The story goes that the sisters made a suicide pact, but not before casting a spell from the *Sixth and Seventh Book of Moses* to curse the land against greed. They stipulated that death would come for anyone who acted on greed on Chickies Rock.[53]

Subsequently, in the decade following this curse, the trolley company ultimately failed, the amusement park was demolished, and in 1896, just a few years after this curse was set, the deadliest trolley accident in Lancaster

---

51. Nicholas A. Tonelli, "2022 Annual Report," Susquehanna River Basin Commission: Coordinating Water Resource Efforts, January 25, 2022, https://web.archive.org/web/20060921133421/http://www.srbc.net/docs/IndianNamesDataChart.PDF.

52. T. M. Berg, W. E. Edmunds, A. R. Geyer, and other compilers, *Geologic Map of Pennsylvania*, 2nd ed., map 1 (Pennsylvania Geologic Survey, 1980), 1:250,000 scale.

53. Adam Zurn, "The Witch Sisters' Chiquesalunga Curse at Chickies Rock," Uncharted Lancaster, October 19, 2019, https://unchartedlancaster.com/2019/10/20/haunted-lancaster-the-witch-sisters-and-chiquesalungas-curse/.

County history happened on Chickies Rock.[54] Now the site is a national park, and no greed is to be had. They don't even charge for parking. The nearest business is a small daycare facility. It seems that the curse has run its course: the sisters ultimately won. And though their time in life was cut short, their spirits seem settled with Chickies Rock now a protected place as a national park.

Sacred sites can develop with use over time as well. Clootie trees are a form of blessing from the land that is found commonly throughout the UK and Ireland. I have had the fortune of tying clootie blessings at Avebury stone circle in England, as well as at a Brigid's Well in County Clare, Ireland. My covenstead in York, Pennsylvania, also has one that we've established over the years.

Exercise: MAKING A CLOOTIE TREE

One of the traditional means of asking for blessing at a sacred site is found in Ireland and the UK: the clootie tree. Clooties are trees or bushes—any size is fine—on which ribbons, fabric, or paper blessings are hung by visitors to ask for healing or offer prayers for themselves or others.

A clootie can be anywhere, but liminal places are great ones. If you have a guardian tree you are working with, perhaps this is a good place for one.

Making a clootie tree can be as simple as designating a site as such, and then allowing your friends, family, and other visitors to hang their blessings upon it. Although it's not a traditional requirement, consider how you can use biodegradable materials that are more respectful to the spirits of place (and require less maintenance for you). Even cooked spaghetti could work in this instance! Or a cardboard ribbon or even a few strands of hair.

If you use nonbiodegradable materials, remove them after a few moon cycles. The intention of the blessing will remain.

---

54. Zurn, "The Witch Sisters' Chiquesalunga Curse."

The next exercise shares how you can consecrate a sacred site, so you can do that at your clootie tree as well if you feel called to.

Establishing Sacred Places

Sacred places don't have to be UNESCO sites. If you made a clootie tree in the previous exercise, you've created a sacred place yourself. People often differentiate between sacred space and a sacred place. Sacred space is usually seen as more temporary, such as a circle cast for a particular ritual on a given day. A sacred place, however, is something permanent and lasting, a place that can be connected to in a meaningful way again and again. You can create sacred sites in these ways:

- *Facilitating the factors that contribute to healing.* This can be collective or personal, such as choosing crystals, imagery, materials, and a location that stimulates healing. This could also look like hosting reiki or other healing ceremonies there. In your cleansing rituals, healing is set as an intention for this space.
- *Dedication to a particular divinity.* Whether that is the land spirits themselves or a god or goddess, dedicating the space to a divinity invites that spirit to join you there. The more work you do in that sacred place with said divinity, the more sacred the place becomes.
- *Deep presence through existence outside of time and space.* Meditation, drum circles, astral travel, trance work, and other out-of-body experiences in a sacred place create what can feel like a vortex of connection. This is what makes certain sacred places feel like portals: they are if we set the intention for them to be.

In essence, we can create sacred places by deepening and continuing our relationship with a sacred space. Every time we assert a space as sacred, such as by hosting rituals there regularly, meditating there, or otherwise engaging with it, we're strengthening its spiritual energy.

We can create sacred places. This can be done intentionally through consecration, ceremony, and repeated action. Newer established sacred sites like Columcille in Bangor, Pennsylvania; the new temple to Apollo in Taranta, Italy; or the Unitarian Universalist Congregation's labyrinth in Frederick, Maryland, have just as much power as the ancient sites they were inspired by. So too are places of repeated sacred activity, like Spiral Sojourn Sanctuary outside York, Pennsylvania, my lineage's covenstead, or Selena Fox's Circle Sanctuary in Barneveld, Wisconsin.

Large sites of significance aren't necessary to create a sacred place. Sanctuaries, shrines, and personal altars can also become sacred sites. Sorita d'Este's Covenant of Hekate has a global list of consecrated shrines to Hekate, and anyone can create and submit one to their directory.[55] You can designate a sacred place anywhere, of any size, with any level of involvement. If it's just for you, that doesn't make it any less powerful; in fact, it might help.

In my experience traveling throughout Europe, the Middle East, India, and North America, the real difference between a sanctuary, temple, shrine, and personal altar is simply size. Though there's no official demarcation, that is the descending order of the size of the space in my own observation.

- Sanctuaries tend to be outdoor places (perhaps also with a temple or shrine on this space), such as a sacred grove, a park, a nature preserve like my lineage's covenstead, or even a festival and event-hosting location like Circle Sanctuary.
- Temples are spaces, usually at least semi-indoors, that again host rituals or events.
- Shrines are smaller, usually communal altars.

All of these are best used communally.

In Japan, shrines and temples are specifically designated as such. In Shinto, followers worship at shrines, and Buddhists worship at temples. Interestingly, most people in Japan practice both religions, because they serve different purposes. A Shinto shrine is the location of earthly matters, where weddings are hosted, or where one would pray for success in life or

55. "COH Sanctuaries," Covenant of Hekate, https://www.hekatecovenant.com/coh-sanctuaries.

business. But Buddhism is the spiritual religion, and so ancestral connections, prayers for spiritual development, and funerals are held at temples.[56]

And then, finally, comes a personal altar. Most people don't see personal altars as sacred places, but I do. I've noticed that even while moving all items away from a space, if an altar has been hosted there, the power of the rituals done leaves a significant imprint on the energy of the place. This, to me, makes altars a powerful opportunity to designate a sacred place. If there's a space outdoors where you often release spell remnants or do magical workings, you might have noticed the land feels different there. Feel for the acceptance or connection from land spirits at these places. If they're accepting, facilitating, or even adding their energy to the workings you're doing, you should be able to feel it. This could be a sacred place in the making already. The following consecration exercise at the end of this chapter can be used to more purposefully designate the sacred place if you're called to do so.

Exercise: CONSECRATING A SACRED PLACE

A consecration is a blessing with stronger, lasting intention behind it. It is a means of spiritually designating an item, place, or person toward a specific end. In my tradition, we're taught consecration of tools as we move through the elements, connecting the tools we use to the deep part of our spiritual selves. The word itself comes from Latin *con-* as in "with, together" and *sacrare*, "to make or declare sacred."[57] This is why I feel a consecration is more than just a blessing: you are forever merging that person, place, or thing with the Divine.

In this case, when we consecrate a sacred place, we're opening up that place as a portal of sorts to connect more deeply and directly with the land spirits and other spirits of place, and perhaps

56. James W. Boyd and Ron G. Williams, "Japanese Shintō: An Interpretation of a Priestly Perspective," *Philosophy East and West* 55, no. 1 (2005): 33, http://www.jstor.org/stable/4487935.

57. Online Etymology Dictionary, "consecration," by Douglas Harper, accessed April 14, 2025, https://www.etymonline.com/word/consecration.

even deities that you might be dedicating this place to. Consecrating a sacred place enhances all magical practice, healing, and ceremony that happens there.

Preparation

Be sure to choose somewhere that won't be easily disturbed. If it is in a publicly accessible place, placing some protective wards as described on page 77 is a good idea.

Once your place has been chosen, do rituals or invite the spirits to connect with you there a few times at least before consecrating it. You can use the meditation Meeting the Spirits of Place, found on page 18. This is a permanent bond, so be sure of it. You will also be responsible for taking care of this area and tending the site, so be sure you're ready to commit fully to this before completing a consecration. Is it a shrine for your backyard that is easily weed-whacked around, or is something indoors better for your abilities?

Decide who will be joining you in this consecration. Will it be a sacred site for the public? For your coven? For your family? Journal these details beforehand, and if others will be involved in this site, they should be involved in the consecration as well.

You don't have to cleanse the space first if it is outdoors, but make sure all items are clean and the space is prepared before beginning (no litter around, the lawn is mowed, etc.).

Timing

I recommend a full moon or on a holiday that aligns with this sacred site. A shrine for Hekate might be best consecrated on the new moon or her feast day, November 16.[58]

Materials Needed

Lighter or matches

Incense (any is fine; I prefer ethically-sourced Tibetan rope incense)

---

58. Prudence Jones, "A Goddess Arrives: Nineteenth Century Sources of the New Age Triple Moon Goddess," *Culture and Cosmos* 9, no. 1 (June 1, 2005): 47–71.

1 cup water from a nearby source, preferably naturally-flowing, but from a hose or sink nearby works too.

1 tablespoon salt. Any kind you prefer is good, but if there is a local salt that is even better.

Candle, big and long-lasting. If this is an outdoor space, you should also consider how to shield the flame from winds that might seek to keep it out. A thick pillar candle in a glass covering would be perfect.

Offerings for the land spirits to be placed in the bowl. Food that is safe to distribute to local wildlife, such as birdseed, is a great choice, as is liquid libation.

Offering bowl or plate that will stay with the shrine, temple, or sanctuary you're consecrating

Hair from participants

Additional offerings for ancestors or deities, if dedicating this sacred place to them (optional)

Other decorations (optional). If dedicating the sacred place to ancestors or deities, bring other statues, pictures of the ancestors, or symbols of the connection you seek to find here. This will also be added to over time.

Directions

1. Place the items on your altar.
2. Turn to the east with your arms raised to the sky and say, "Guardians of the East, Element of Air, creatures of wing and sky, I invite your blessings to witness the consecration of this shrine/temple/sanctuary. May healing and connection find us here, and may your winds of protection blow away any who seek to harm this shrine/temple/sanctuary. Hail and welcome."
3. Turn to the south with your arms raised in front of you, palms open, and say, "Guardians of the South, Element of Fire, creatures of heat and poison, I invite your blessings of desire and passion. May this be a space for expansive growth and realizations of joy. Hail and welcome."

4. Turn to the west with your arms out to your sides, palms open, and say, "Guardians of the West, Element of Water, creatures of sea and river, lake and ocean, I invite your blessings of loving relationships and the flow of natural emotions. May this be a place of powerful relationships between humans and spirits. Hail and welcome."
5. Turn to the north with your arms palms down to the earth and say, "Guardians of the North, Element of our Mother Earth, creatures of wood and field, I invite your blessings of stability and grounding to our shrine. May your presence aid us in building a solid foundation of protection and connection here. Hail and welcome."
6. Standing facing your altar, begin placing the offerings into the bowl and say, "Spirits of this land, I invite your blessings to this shrine. Be present with us, and protect this space as you do this land. May this shrine, dedicated in the name of [any deities, the ancestors, or perhaps the land spirits themselves], [names of all those present in the consecration], and myself [your name and title, if applicable], be blessed, protected, and connected when here in this sacred place. May this be a place of deep love and connection to you and all spirits of the sacred wild. May it be so." Lift the bowl full of offerings up to the land, and then place it back on the altar.
7. Optionally, invoke any deities you will dedicate this space to, if any. If you're planning on doing ancestral work here extensively, such as having an ancestor altar here, invite the Honored Dead to join you as well. This is as simple as saying, "Honored Dead/Goddess Aphrodite/etc., I invite you to inhabit and bless this space of sacred connection to your gifts of [what you love about connecting with them]." Give your offerings to them if you planned to invite them.
8. Once all spirits have been called in, light the incense. Waft the smoke over the people present, the items, and the full size of

the space. Repeat as you do so, "Powers of air and fire, bless this space with your gifts of awareness and inspiration, passion and purpose. Bring us your lessons in this time of new beginnings."

9. Sprinkle the water at each person and over the space and on each item. "Life-giving water, I invite your blessings of cleansing and purification. Bring us your lesson of learning to flow with change."
10. Sprinkle the salt at each person, over the space, and onto each item. "Grounding earth, our Mother, bless us with your all-knowing serenity. Bring us your lesson of stability."
11. Now light the candle. "As the flame is to the candle, may it be the soul of this space. Spirits of place and land, we thank you for your welcome. [Deity invoked, if any], we thank you for your presence. [If you have invited ancestors, more deities, etc., thank them as well.]"
12. Pass the offering plate through the flame to imbue it with this energy. Place the plate down where it will rest in the sacred place. "We consecrate this space in the name of [say your name, the coven's name, or names of all present]." Next, have each person place their hair in the bowl themselves or blow over the offering, and individually state, "I consecrate this space in the name of [their name or the coven's name]."
13. Now the space is consecrated! Feel free to make more connection here today. Run a meditation for those present, drum, sing, create art, journal, or move on.
14. Release the elements in reverse order.
    a. Turn to the north with your arms palms down to the earth and say, "Guardians of the North, Element of our Mother Earth, creatures of wood and field, thank you for your blessings of stability and grounding. Go if you must; stay if you will. Hail and farewell."
    b. Turn to the west with your arms out to your sides, palms open, and say, "Guardians of the West, Element of Water,

creatures of sea and river, lake and ocean, thank you for your blessings of loving relationships and the flow of natural emotions. Go if you must; stay if you will. Hail and farewell."

c. Turn to the south with your arms raised in front of you, palms open, and say, "Guardians of the South, Element of Fire, creatures of heat and poison, thank you for your blessings of desire and passion. Go if you must; stay if you will. Hail and farewell."

d. Turn to the east with your arms raised to the sky and say, "Guardians of the East, Element of Air, creatures of wing and sky, thank you for your blessings to witness the consecration of this shrine/temple/sanctuary. Go if you must; stay if you will. Hail and farewell."

Leave the hair on the plate as an offering, and after some time (three days or so), if it's still there, take it to the nearest point outdoors from the space for birds to take for their nests or bury it in your garden or houseplants to nurture the soil. If there is a sacred plant in the newly consecrated sacred place, you can also bury the hair there.

Repeat this consecration if you are passing the torch to a new keeper of the space or priest/ess/ex. When the candle is near death, light the new candle from the old to maintain the same energy of the sacred place. Alternatively, if you want to shift the energy in a big way, you might want to start fresh with the candle's energy, but this would be a very extreme circumstance, such as breaking ties with the person who began said shrine or if there were really sinister things that happened at the site.

Ley Lines

For some who follow the study of ley lines, ley lines provide a clear explanation of the existence of sacred sites. Ley lines are thought to be horizontal lines circling and crossing the earth, and some people believe that sacred sites are built upon them either on purpose or by the creator being drawn by the energy of the ley lines to create a sacred site there. The term *ley line* was first coined by Alfred Watkins in 1920.[59] Watkins was a follower of the Earth Mysteries movement, an archaeological movement that is often followed by those on pagan paths. The Earth Mysteries movement concerns itself with looking for syncretic universality in global spiritual traditions for answers on the great mysteries of the earth and our many civilizations. The movement, in a too-short definition, teaches that the ancient cultures of the world—from Greece to India to China and down to South America—had an understanding of the spiritual lines that crossed the earth, almost like rubber bands around a baseball. And with this knowledge, they built sacred sites at these places.

At the back of the book in the recommended reading section, you'll find more books to dive into if the Earth Mysteries movement tickles your magical fancy. Be aware, however, that ley lines can be controversial. Scientists by and large have claimed that they don't exist, as they've never been able to measure or find them.[60] For me, they are a means to an end when working with land spirits, as they give context and a vocabulary to discuss the way the earth's energies can be experienced.

Ley lines, to me, can be a modern method of conceptualizing land spirits. Just like a ley line, land spirits are stationary in their place. If this is an understanding of spirit of place that resonates with you, it can certainly be understood from that lens. Words are human constructs; when we label things or give meaning to something with a specific term or word, it is to better communicate it to others and to more strongly signal identity to ourselves and others. Labels on our spiritual path are always about what works for us.

In India, though no Hindu practitioners I've ever come across use the term *ley lines*, there is a practice in Hinduism of finding the "spiritual center" of the earth that does flow in a line when building new temples. It involves using bells and vibratory incantations to call to the spirits and deities for advice on where to build a temple. This was told to me by my tour

---

59. Clive Ruggles, *Ancient Astronomy: An Encyclopedia of Cosmologies and Myth* (ABC-CLIO, 2005), 224.

60. Ruggles, *Ancient Astronomy*, 225.

guide at the temples of Khajuraho in Northern India. Interestingly, these temples are said to be built on ley lines by those who study ley lines.

The Mystery of Sacred Sites

Sacred sites are mysterious, and we don't have to fully understand them. The Earth Mysteries will likely never be solved fully, unless we figure out time travel and a way to communicate effectively with people from the past. But the experience of them is real, and that's what counts. Explanation is only a small part of our soul journey: experience is the lion's share of the pagan path. In your journey with land spirits, make it a priority to experience sacred places, create sacred space, dabble in connection in new and various ways, and find your own understanding of what makes a place sacred.

Meditation: CONNECTING TO SACRED SITES

This meditation is best performed at a sacred site. As I described, this location doesn't have to be in guidebooks or internet searches for sacred sites, but it should be somewhere you can go safely and connect deeply with the energy of the land spirits. You can start with online research if you're drawing a blank for accessible sacred sites near you, but if a place came to you right away, that's the best place to go.

If this is your first time at this site, spend time exploring and introducing yourself to the land spirits before engaging in this activity. If you've been to this location before, a quick introduction and announcement of yourself at this space is all you need. I recommend bringing an offering—this can be as simple as water from your bottle or a snack you brought that's safe for the animals around the area to eat. Once you've offered your offering, find yourself a comfortable, out-of-the-way spot to sit and connect to the energy of the site. Ideally, this is somewhere people won't stare at you or find themselves curious or connecting their energy to yours through observation.

Draw your attention to your breathing, inhaling deeply through your nose and exhaling fully also through your nose. Inhale into your diaphragm, feeling your lungs expand, and exhale fully yet slowly. Continuing your steady, even inhales and exhales through your nose, keep your eyes open. We will move through your senses, beginning with what you can see. Recall what you saw as you first entered the site. Remember what you saw at the site before sitting down. Take in what's in front of you, then behind you; to your right and to your left. If you know what's beyond your immediate vision, try to picture that too. Now steady your breathing again and close your eyes.

What do you hear? Match the sounds to their origins if you can. What do you smell? Again, consider if you can name those scents and where they're coming from. What does it feel like to be sitting on this ground? Press your hands into the ground and touch the grass or other plants, soil, or rocks beneath you.

Now, holding your hands palms down to the earth beside your body, steady your breathing once more. What can you feel in your spiritual body? What are the emerging emotions of the land beneath and around you? How does it make you feel emotionally to be here? Take your time with this.

After some time, you should be able to assess how you feel at this site, if it's welcoming, positive energy or not. If you are feeling energized, uplifted, excited, happy, or calmer than you did before you came here, proceed to the next part of the meditation. If you're feeling heavier, sadder, unsettled, or tired, thank the land spirits for their attention and open your eyes. I recommend shielding your energy as well before leaving the space.

If the energy is positive, you now have the option to deepen your connection to the spirits there. Focus your own energy through your palms and into the land. Imagine your love and calm flowing from your heart, out to your shoulders, and down your arms. Picture how it makes your arms seem to glow. Feel the warmth of this loving, kind energy of welcome. Focus on your connection to the land here: give gratitude for the chance to be here.

Now that you've sent some of your own positive energy, allow the flow to reverse. Picture a gentle, equally warm flow of glowing energy emerging from the ground and up into your hands. As this energy reaches your palm, accept it into your body. You'll start to glow again in your arms, this time extending the warm, golden light of the sacred place's energy up to your shoulders.

Let it flow through you, heading upward and downward in your body simultaneously, warming and alighting you throughout. As this warm glow reaches across your throat chakra, it branches both upward and downward. It flows down, filling your heart, torso, and solar plexus, making your sides tingle with connection. Let it flow down to your sacral chakra and your root and along the full length of your legs to the tips of your toes.

As the other branch of light continues up through your head and out your crown, let this love and calm flow out of you and back to the egregore of the sacred place. You are a conduit for spiritual connection. As this flow continues for a few moments, let yourself be recharged. Hold on to this feeling so that you can astrally project yourself here again in the future as needed.

CHAPTER 9
Spirit-Led Travel

There's a whole world of land spirits outside your door. You can build meaningful relationships with them wherever you are, and they can be powerful allies for everything from protection magic to shadow work. Seeking Numina, meaning "seeking places of spiritual power," is my business's name because that has been my life's calling. I grew up in the United States, moved to Bahrain as a teenager, and then moved to Greece as an adult. Living on three continents, I have also traveled extensively through the Middle East, Europe, and North America. And I've gone almost everywhere following the guidance of my spirit team and the land spirits that call me to them.

Spirit-led travel is a path you set foot on. It's a different mindset to approach the world with. Instead of choosing places to travel based on what looks good on social media or cheap flight deals or because it's simply what you've heard of, spirit-led travel is what it sounds like: it's letting spirit guide your next trip. The first time I used the term *spirit-led travel* was in a conversation with my friend. She was asking why I went to Switzerland recently. It wasn't high on my list, it isn't cheap, and it felt really random to her.

In explaining the call I got—the signs I followed, the disconnect I felt when I didn't lean toward this new direction—I said, "It's like I was being led by spirit," and that's when it clicked.

I had been, every step of the way.

When I moved to Greece, I got a lot of indications that I was supposed to embrace a new part of myself. In all my meditation and divination, the lion kept coming up. I'm a Leo rising, so I figured maybe I need to lean into that. As I did, it felt uncomfortable but not wrong—like I was growing into a new role. I remember thinking to myself, "I'm open to Leo lessons." This quickly became a mantra. That's when I started seeing the Lucerne lion statue. Then someone brought up Lauterbrunnen. Then I turned on a podcast, and one of the hosts digressed to talking about St. Beatus Caves. Then my brother told me about Interlaken. Then the lion statue came up, again and again in weird and unexpected contexts. This wasn't just an algorithm directing me. I realized this lion's journey would take me on a new type of vacation to experience lands that were calling to me.

In Lion's true energy, I learned to rest and relax, but also to stand up for myself and push myself toward new challenges. As I traveled the land of Switzerland, I met land spirits in all the places I mentioned, and they pushed me out of my comfort zone and into personal growth. As I built trust with these new land spirits, I felt more confident to try out physical activities that might have seemed too intense had I not been on a spiritual path of challenging myself already. Hiking the Alps, tackling my fear of heights, riding bikes in difficult terrain over long distances, and navigating the scale and length of travel on the European train system I had never encountered. I traveled all over the country and even dipped into Germany. Most importantly, I learned how to lean into my own inner lion energy: how to use charisma and communication. I learned to know when to pause and think and when to act and make things happen.

Spirit-led travel is about letting yourself trust the process and be guided even when it seems strange or impractical. This trip was manifested for me but also by me, as I chose to tune in to these lessons along the way. I chose to lean into the teachings of the land spirits. To listen, deeply, to what they could teach me. This has been the theme of all my trips to seemingly random places. And by keeping open and trusting in my guides and the land spirits they introduce me to, I've known I'm on the right path the whole time.

Why Travel?

Spirit-led travel builds trust between you and your spiritual path. When the things you are manifesting are happening in more than just your private moments in controlled, familiar environments, it feels more powerful because it seems less likely. Because you're in an unfamiliar environment, you're also more attuned to the experiences you have. You're more likely to notice signs because you're naturally more aware of your surroundings in new places.

Spirit-led travel also asks you to trust in big ways. The investment, the time and energy of travel, and the challenges it might bring up are all offerings to the land spirits you're seeking to connect with on a trip to somewhere new. It is a big trust exercise with the universe to embark on spirit-led travel. It's always expansive and worth these sacrifices, and in fact, the sacrifices of time and money are the ways we show our commitment to the lessons we're being invited to receive when we're led somewhere new. I've built connections and friendships with land spirits all over the world because of this trust.

Fears of Travel

Travel is a fast pass to personal growth. When we travel to new cultures and countries, hearing languages that are not our own, seeing a way of life we don't relate to (at least at first), eating new foods and smelling new smells, our minds open new pathways reclaiming our childlike wonder. Neuroplasticity is the concept that the brain learns and grows, including when we must navigate new places.[61] Travel is the ultimate way of exploring a new place. It's not just a figure of speech. Your mind is literally changed by travel.

So if you view that through a spiritual lens, the possibilities for growth are endless. Shadow work and epiphanies about your path come naturally when conquering yourself by embracing new challenges in a new environment. That's the key: a new environment with new challenges. That's what

---

61. Jessica Koehler, "The Transcendent Power of Travel," *Psychology Today*, October 19, 2024, https://www.psychologytoday.com/us/blog/beyond-school-walls/202410/the-transcendent-power-of-travel.

defines travel, in my mind. You don't have to travel far. Going to your first spiritual conference, a workshop, or a retreat a few hours away still counts.

But whenever we are confronted with an opportunity for growth like this, it can be natural for the ego to feel a bit threatened. Anything that feels like a disturbance in the status quo can be perceived as a threat to the ego. And this can stop us in our tracks. It is important to manage and confront your fears of traveling so that you can make the most of the opportunity travel is.

What part of your shadow is threatened by travel? These feelings likely arose as you've been reading this chapter. Does travel feel too exotic for you and your life? Perhaps it feels selfish or frivolous to even think about travel. Is there a bitterness you have about the costs of travel? What are the automatic *no*s rising when you begin to think about travel? Journal these feelings in your magical journal.

Remember that these feelings are coming from your ego, not necessarily your truth. Our ego sees change as a threat because it's different. Your ego means well; it's just trying to protect you from unknowns. But pushing our comfort zone is part of that necessary journey of growth. Where is your ego trying to control you? Why do you think there's a resistance to travel? Are you ready to release these anxieties and limiting beliefs?

And if you do release these limiting beliefs, what could happen? Direct this thought experiment down a positive path. What do you stand to gain if you lean into travel and meeting new land spirits? Consider journaling on this idea.

Exercise: ADDRESSING FEARS OF TRAVEL

Do some fear-setting. If you're not sure if you want to travel but know that you should, or if you can feel that it would be good for you if you could just get over those fears, this is the exercise for you. Fear-setting, pioneered by Tim Ferriss, is like goal-setting, but instead you look for all the things that can go wrong and brainstorm the ways they could go right. Resources are available for free online about this, including worksheets.[62] I recommend doing it every time you have a decision to make, and eventually, it becomes a useful lens you can use to look at anything that comes your way.

If you're having trouble getting started, begin a journaling session with "My biggest fears about traveling are..." This might be better reflected on as a mind map, or even a freewrite, in which you write unimpeded for a certain amount of time on the subject. Getting all these fears to the surface is the key, and then you can begin addressing the worst-case scenarios if they were to come true. More times than not, this leaves us realizing it's worth facing those fears.

Avoiding Homesickness

Many people are afraid to travel because of homesickness. If you've begun any of the exercises or mediations presented so far in this book, you've found that the land spirits have proven themselves to be fantastic allies of protection and personal growth. You can bring this grounding energy of stability and home with you wherever you go and work with the land spirits of your home to alleviate your homesickness.

Affirmational blessings, giving gratitude for home, and remembering why this trip is so important to you help reframe homesickness. Before you leave, take a picture of the vision board you'll create later in this chapter. Remind yourself of the affirmation you created for this trip.

And last, make sure you do your pre-trip protection work. Refresh your wards and ask the land spirits to keep an eye on things while you're gone. Even though they probably would anyway, letting them in on it will give you peace of mind.

Talismans from home are the best way to literally bring a bit of home with you on your spirit-led travel. When you make a witch's ladder, incorporate things from your home, asking your land spirits to provide you with a rock, acorn, or other item. This is a powerful tool to bring with you on a trip. You can also create an impresa, an emblem of your home, that you can carry with you.

---

62. Tim Ferriss, "Fear-Setting: The Most Valuable Exercise I Do Every Month," *Tim Ferriss* (blog), May 15, 2017, https://tim.blog/2017/05/15/fear-setting/.

Exercise: CREATING AN IMPRESA

Impresa is another word for an emblem of something or a coat of arms for a family. This impresa will be a natural element that reminds you of home: the coat of arms of your land spirits. It can be anything, from the simple to the intricate. You can get ornate with it, such as weaving a small coaster using dried grasses from your land or even making a small broom or plant bundle. Or you can ask your land spirits for a totem of home, such as an acorn, a rock, or a small chip of wood. A vial of herbs, perhaps a tiny jar you can wear as a necklace, is a great option too. If you have a flower or leaf from home pressed in the back of your phone case, you already have a functioning impresa.

Materials Needed

Item that will serve as your impresa
Offering to the land spirits

Directions

1. Bring your item to your land spirits altar at home. Give your offering to the land spirits and thank them for their love, protection, and connection.
2. Hold the impresa to the ground under your hand and say, "My home is safe. My land is minded. While I'm away, may only love and peace find it."
3. Pick up the item, hold it to your heart, and say, "My heart is with this land. My home is safe. My land is minded. While I'm away, may only love and peace find it."
4. Pick up the item, hold it to the sky, and say, "No matter where I travel, my home is safe. My land is minded. While I'm away, may only love and peace find it."
5. Leave it on your land spirits altar to charge, or pack it with your witch's ladder (see page 163) and journal. It is ready.

6. Repeat these words to yourself when you're traveling and feeling anxious about home, holding the impresa to your heart or to the sky as you do so. This is both an affirmation and a blessing, further protecting your home while you're away even as it alleviates homesickness.

When you're on your trip, sleep with it under your pillow to ground yourself back home again. Whenever homesickness strikes, hold it in your hand and remember the experience of finding it. Remember what it felt like to be surrounded by your land and held by it as it led you to this item. And remember too that you'll be home before you know it.

Why a Place Calls Us

There are a lot of nuanced reasons why a particular place might be calling to you. Sometimes it's for the lessons only the land spirits of that place can teach you. Certain land spirits are excellent for releasing attachments; other land spirits have a deep gift for absolving fears. Other times it's to connect to something deeper in your spiritual work, such as ancestry. It can also be that the energy of that place has a certain gift that you need to receive, such as the healing at a hot spring or being called to visit the temple of a deity you've worked with for years. The land spirits are the undercurrent of each of these places. Recognizing that you are being invited to join them in their home is a gift unlike any other.

Astrocartography

A place may call to you because of your astromap, or the map of where the lines of your astrological birth chart fall across the earth. Your astromap shows certain places where your astrology might indicate a good place to live, start a career, meet your partner, or other things astrology can help you understand. Astrocartography, the study of astromaps, adds a layer of location to your chart. Knowing where a place you're visiting is in your astromap is a good way to introduce yourself to a new spirit of place. They might already be expecting you.

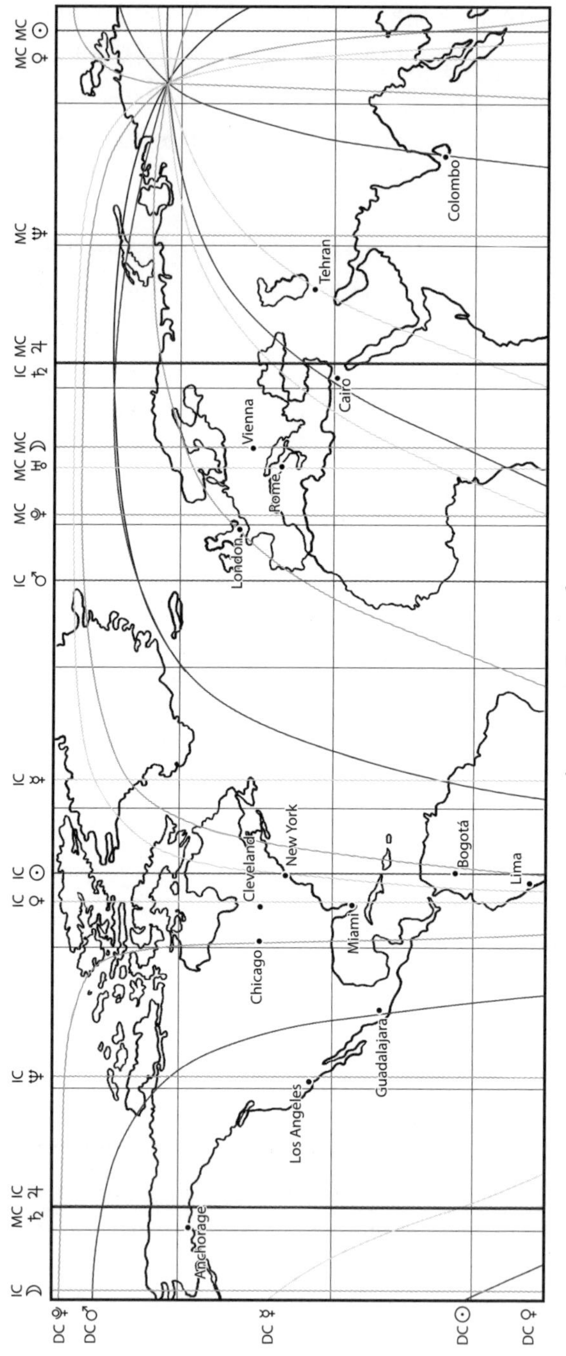

Astromap Example

The places we grow up, move to, visit often, or simply feel a connection to even if we haven't visited usually have something significant in our astromap. This is a map of the world that our birth chart overlays directly on top of, and where the lines of our chart go through certain places indicates how that place will or won't agree with us.

The astromap example on the previous page shows data for a person born in New York City, January 1, 1970, at 12:00 am. You can see there are lines going through different locations. The person's sun goes directly through New York City, where they were born, indicating that New York City is likely a place where they will feel seen and understood and be able to live up to their potential. I also see that they have a Venus line moving through Ohio—maybe they will have to travel somewhere along that line to meet their life partner. These are just examples.

I am not an astrocartographer, so I can't go into the depth that I recommend you pursue. I did have my own chart read, and it was eye-opening. I recommend finding a professional who can do this for you so that you can properly read what you're seeing, though there are online programs that can create one for you. With websites like Astro-Seek, it is fun to take a look and see what you can find.[63] It might help you understand why you do or don't feel at home where you currently live.

It's my belief that when we come into this world, we choose our astrology from the other side. In a way, it's our clue to the mission of this life. We can find clues to our mission in this life all over, from divination to the spiritual callings we feel at different times toward different tasks. But astrology is a lifelong guide I definitely recommend exploring.

Ancestor Connection

One's ancestry is the cultural and historical background that formed them. Ancestral lands are anywhere that was formative and important for your family, chosen family, or even spiritual lineage throughout history. Many people are descended from adopted families, enslaved ancestry, or cultures with limited bookkeeping. My dad is Greek-Egyptian and was born in

---

63. "AstroCartography, Astro Map," Astro-Seek, accessed November 25, 2024, https://horoscopes.astro-seek.com/astrocartography-online-astro-map-relocation.

Egypt. In Egypt, it's not customary to digitize old records, so he couldn't find anything beyond the word of mouth from his family members even if he wanted to. His birthday isn't even known. No one recorded the date. In those days, people gave birth at home and then had to go in person to the nearest government offices to register, which was many miles away, so it wasn't done in a timely manner. These disconnects from your blood relatives may be some of the trauma the land will heal with you. Visiting these places or connecting to them in the ways you can will be a helpful way of connecting to your ancestry.

Many people the world over are unable to live in their home countries due to financial or safety issues. In the United States, Canada, Australia, and New Zealand especially, most people living there aren't living in countries where their ancestry is from, and they likely haven't been for generations. Much of the migration to these countries has historically been due to economic hardship and seeking asylum. This trauma of being forced to leave one's ancestral homeland is something spirit-led travel can invite you to heal by visiting those ancestral lands.

Feeling lost or disconnected from our heritage isn't easy, and it is natural to feel an inclination toward visiting the countries of our ancestry. Your ancestors might call to you from the place of their birth.

The spirits of place are a big draw for those of us curious about our historical homelands. If you can find the places your ancestors directly shipped out from or an ancestral place you'd like to travel to, start connecting to the real sites at those places.

Get on Google Maps and use Street View to walk the same streets your ancestors may have walked. What does it look like? Do any feelings arise as you "walk" the streets? Record your experiences in your land spirits journal.

If you plan to travel to this place, remember this first encounter with it and compare your experiences when your feet are actually there on the ground. Did it feel like you expected? Again, add these thoughts to your journal.

If you're drawn to spirit-led travel involving ancestors, especially individual people in your lineage, visiting their final resting place is a powerful way to connect. The land spirits there have welcomed their bodies, and their bodies have become one with the land in which they're buried. The land spirits are literally holding space for your ancestors. This exercise is one you can host at the cemetery or gravesite of any loved one who has passed away or on their ancestral lands.

Exercise: HOSTING AN AGAPE TABLE

When you travel to the burial lands of your ancestors, consider hosting an agape table. An agape table is similar to a dumb supper. *Agape* (*ah-GAH-pee*) is the Greek word for "love," and agape tables were tables carved of stone inside family tombs and catacombs where family members would gather on memorials or birthdays to have a feast in celebration of that person.[64] Found in Malta but tied to the Roman conquest of the island, this is an open practice with an unclear lineage. Feel free to make it your own. Building a stone table might not be an option, but consider having a picnic at the site of your ancestors' burial. Invite other family members if it feels relevant, and serve a plate for the ancestor you wish to connect to. When you invite them to dine with you, they can also give you messages and connect with you at the table (or on your picnic blanket).

Before You Travel

You can start to connect to the land spirits you'll meet on your spirit-led trip even before you travel. This prepares you mentally and emotionally for the trip, especially if you're a nervous traveler. The meditation at the end of the chapter is also a great way to ground and center those nerves in preparation.

The first step, beyond the necessary mundane things like making sure your pets and plants have care, your locks all work, and so on, is refreshing your protection magic and alerting your local land spirits before you travel. You can set new wards if you feel called to, or you can simply do a cleansing of the property. Always let your land spirits know if someone

---

64. Eric C. Smith, "The History of the Catacombs," in *Foucault's Heterotopia in Christian Catacombs* (Palgrave Macmillan, 2014), 5–14.

might be coming by that they're not used to in order to check on things while you're gone. Let them know your plans and schedule, even if they won't follow a calendar to know exactly when you'll be back. Keeping them in the loop is the key.

Being spirit-led doesn't mean not thinking—it usually means thinking a whole lot more. Some shadow work and looking within is what led you to this trip, so as you plan the mundane details like where to have a layover and what number seat to choose, let your intuition guide you. It's always a good idea to get the mundane details like bookings and tickets figured out before you go. You don't want anything stressing you out while you travel. So inviting the energy of the place you're traveling to into your life in the months leading up to the trip is a great way to prepare to meet the land spirits there.

You don't have to overplan your trip. Let yourself be guided while you travel. No need to pick out every restaurant months before your trip! But certain places do sell out of tickets, sometimes months in advance, so being aware of that is important. Once the mundane details, the planning, and the protection magic have been done, you'll want to set some goals for this trip. Don't put too much pressure on these goals, but keep in mind the shadow work and self-reflection that led to this journey.

Exercise: SPIRIT-LED TRAVEL VISION BOARD

In this exercise, you'll get creative, making a vision board about the place you're being called to visit. Even if you aren't planning the trip yet, this exercise will act as a means of manifesting the trip you dream of.

Materials Needed

Poster board (any size)
Printed photos or maps of the place you aim to travel
Pens and markers (colors optional, but have fun with this!)

Directions

1. In the center of your poster board, write an affirmation for this trip. The first place that comes to mind when you think about traveling is probably the place you're being called to the most. What would you hope to learn from visiting there? What realizations or healing would you embrace? This is the key to finding your affirmation. Some examples are "I am connected to my ancestors" if you aim to travel to ancestral lands, and "I release the pain of my divorce." If you have no particular goals, something to affirm your mindset in regard to the trip, like "I embrace the wisdom of Ireland's land spirits," is a good way to go.
2. Surround the affirmation with photos, maps, and other drawings or decorations you choose to add. Enjoy the process. As you create your vision board, think about the trip or even put on a documentary or podcast about traveling to that place. Let your mind connect to the spirit of that place.
3. Hang the board where you'll see it, perhaps above your desk at work or at your altar. When you see it, focus on the things you dream of doing in that place: picture yourself eating that gelato by the Trevi Fountain in Rome or walking the path up to the Acropolis in Athens.

The more time you spend visualizing and connecting to the place, the more you'll be called to it, and the more likely this trip is to happen because you're directing your energy toward it. You can start saving part of each paycheck a little at a time toward this trip, and no matter how long it takes to manifest, the vision board will keep you on track to making it happen.

What to Bring on a Spirit-Led Pilgrimage

When packing for a spirit-led trip, there's no special tools you need to bring to get the most out of your experience besides your spiritual mindset. But I do recommend bringing a journal or your favorite way to record your experiences. If you're a photographer or videographer, bring that equipment, but again, don't put too much pressure on the trip if that isn't your thing. Bringing your magical journal is sufficient.

Also, bring any spiritual items you want to charge at the magical places you're visiting. This could be jewelry, your tarot cards, a tool that's safe to travel with (no athames, sadly), or even an altar cloth. You can leave these items out while you meditate in connection to the sacred sites, or touch them to sacred relics or items if it's allowed. I bring my tarot cards with me, charge them at the base of temples in Greece, and bring them to my favorite places even if I know I won't be giving readings just so they'll soak up the energy of the land spirits there.

If you're prone to homesickness, bring a tangible, physical item from your land spirits at home. More on that in this chapter's section on homesickness.

You also might want to bring materials needed for a travel altar, especially if you'll be away for a holiday or other observance such as a full moon and don't want to miss it. Travel altars are small kits that allow you to perform magic on the go. Many I've seen include simply a small candle, incense, matches, and a crystal good for most connection like quartz. These can be boxes that you open and everything you need is inside: a portable altar in a box. It also can be a magical toolkit of items you bring with you to create an altar in your hotel room while you're traveling.

I find the connection is more important than replicating a ritual out in nature, especially since working with open flame is usually not permissible at sacred sites or in busy places. My travel altar is a witch's ladder, a rosary of sorts made of important items and symbols of your spiritual path, and gifts from the land spirits. I consider it an altar because it has every ingredient of an altar at home—a representation of each element, my lineage in my coven, and gifts from sacred sites I was called to add to it. I use it to ground and connect in the morning just like I would at my altar, but it is small and easy to bring with to sacred sites where I can bless it as well, continuing to build its power.

Exercise: MAKING A WITCH'S LADDER

A witch's ladder is an ideal travel altar, in my opinion, because it can have everything you would want on your altar. It's small and simple and requires no setup, so I'm more likely to find time and energy to use it while I'm traveling. It's also inconspicuous, allowing me to use it for connection to the land spirits anywhere I want to connect with them.

Simply put, a witch's ladder is like a rosary made of items that are significant to you instead of just beads. I used excess cords from my initiation for my current witch's ladder, but any hardy yarn or string will do. Choosing a color significant to your spiritual journey is a good start, such as red for life and protection, white for clarity and purity, pink for self-love, purple for psychic awareness, blue for calm and peace, and black for shadow work or connection to the veil.

You also need items of spiritual significance to attach to the string. These can be anything, and whatever significance matters most to your spiritual path: for example, one item for each element and an item for each deity. I have a representation of each element, a clear quartz to remind me to walk with clarity everywhere I travel, and a pendant from my family to remind me of my ancestors and to keep that connection open. I also have a pendant from my high priestess on it to remember my spiritual ancestors.

If you're at a loss for what items to include, go ask the land spirits. They'll provide the gifts you need. You also can start small and add to it like a charm bracelet while you travel. Charm bracelets are called such for a reason!

Materials Needed

2 feet of yarn

3–7 items to tie into the witch's ladder

Incense

Offering to the land spirits

Note: I like to use Tibetan rope incense as it leaves no trace, but anything cleansing like cedar, sandalwood, sage, rosemary, or lavender is a great choice.

Directions

1. Take the ingredients outside to your land spirits altar or favorite guardian. Light the incense and tell the land spirits you're making an altar to take with you on adventures.
2. Pass each item through the smoke of the incense one at a time, starting with the yarn. Set an intention with each item, saying why you picked it.
3. After everything has been cleansed in the incense smoke, begin tying the items into the string one by one, focusing on why you're adding each item to strengthen this intention. Leave some room at the end of your witch's ladder to add more items in the future.
4. Once it's made, offer your offering to the land spirits and thank them for joining you in creating this witch's ladder. Pass the finished ladder through the smoke again three times, and it's ready to go. You can optionally leave it to charge on your land spirits altar, but it is now ready to be packed for your trip.

You can use a witch's ladder like any other spiritual tool, by calling each element in on individual items hanging on it or designating each charm to a specific purpose. Sometimes using my travel altar looks like holding it while I meditate at a sacred site or while I look up at the moon. That's the benefit of a witch's ladder: it's small and simple to take with you anywhere. If you're traveling during a full moon, leaving it to bask under the same moon in a new place is a great way to charge it with the intention of spirit-led travel too.

I also keep my witch's ladder in a small bag that holds little trinkets that won't fit on a witch's ladder but that I want to carry around with me. Inside, I've added a dried olive from the oldest olive tree in Greece—too fragile to put on the ladder but strong enough to carry in the bag.

Introducing Yourself to New Land Spirits

The land spirits in a new place will have a different feeling, and they'll be your key to getting to know this new place. It's the spirits of the land that draw us, usually, even if it's the egregore of the city you're being called to, or its history or landmark events. Learning how to get in touch with these new spirits is the first step to making the most of a spirit-led adventure. I usually do this by simply meditating. The meditation on page 35 to receive the name of the land is a good introductory meditation, as is the meditation on page 146 to connect to sacred sites. Bring an offering, and in crowded places, be prepared to first meet the egregore. This might be a good time to start with the egregore exercise on page 120. In places with a more open landscape around them, the energy can be overwhelming because it's so palpable and different from what you're used to. Meditation and contemplation, slowing down and taking your time, are key to getting the most out of the experience.

This connection isn't just for connecting to sacred places, although, as discussed in chapter 8, be careful not to hold a narrow definition of what that means. If you are being led somewhere, there's a reason. Connect where you're called to. For example, York, Pennsylvania, has an energy I can't resist. Anyone from that area always rolls their eyes or looks at me with disbelief when I say that, but it's true. The land there speaks to me. I've written sacred poetry about the way it feels to drive the winding country roads along the Codorus Creek, an offshoot of the Susquehanna. It wasn't until I did more research into the lore and spiritual history of the Susquehanna River and the Susquehannock and Lenape tribes that I found any "evidence" for why I felt so connected, but I still connected then, and I still do whenever I am in the US because it just calls to me.

The difference between meeting land spirits while traveling and meeting them when you're stationary at home is, of course, time. You won't have as much time with these new land spirits, perhaps only an hour or two, so you might have to work a bit faster. The good thing is your growth mindset will be ignited by the act of traveling, and you'll be able to connect more deeply much quicker. This is why having a spirit-led mindset when you travel is so helpful: you're staying in a state of openness, and the universe will, in a sense, do the rest.

Once you've introduced yourself and given an offering, you can begin a deeper connection to this place, so you can internalize its power. You should immediately feel a kinship or not when you visit a place because getting spiritual callings for that particular place was the start of this bond. If this feels like somewhere you want to feel a connection to even after you leave, it's a good idea to create a bond by leaving some of your hair.

If you know you want to take a bit of this place with you, do so with care. A great way to create this bond is to place some of your hair in offering at the place that feels right, such as the threshold, or maybe even bury it gently if the site has lots of grass or exposed ground.

Exercise: SISTER CITY BOND

The following exercise is something I only recommend when you really, truly want a lifelong connection to a particular place. A sister city bond might only be something you do once or twice in all your life. I've only ever created a sister city bond between Pennsylvania and Greece, two places I call home. You'll need to be prepared before you leave for your trip as well, because the key is swapping dirt between these countries. It's important that you only bring a tiny, modicum amount of dirt with you from your home, and only take the same tiny amount home with you. We're talking the amount of a teaspoon, just enough to sprinkle a few times. If anyone asks at airport security, tell them it's a spiritual talisman and this is usually sufficient to allow your passage. As always, follow your own moral compass if this feels uncomfortable. Bringing a seashell, a small rock, or another natural item from a place you want to create a sister city bond with is effective, but I personally feel dirt, as the essence of place, is the best choice.

Materials Needed

Spoon (at home and at the sacred site)

Container for the dirt from home (a small jar or plastic baggie will be sufficient)

Offering to the land spirits at home (I recommend hair.)
Offering to the land spirits at the sacred place (I recommend hair.)

Directions

1. Before you leave for the trip, go to your land spirits altar or guardian with a spoon or shovel, your container, and an offering. Ask if you can take some dirt with you. Leave your offering, and when you feel their assent, scoop some dirt into the container.
2. On your trip, when you find a place you want to have a sister city bond with, take a spoon, the dirt from home, and an offering. Find a location at the site where you won't be disturbed.
3. Leave your offering to the land and ask if they want to bond with you. You should feel the land receive this with a gentle breeze rising up around you; birds, frogs, crickets, cicadas, or other animals singing a bit more brightly; or even a beautiful flower or butterfly making itself known.
4. When you have your sign of acceptance, use the spoon to dig a small hole and pour in the dirt from home. Add your hair or other offering to this hole.
5. Using your spoon, dig up a little dirt and put it in the container you came with.

When you get home, keep this dirt on your altar. It can form the foundations of spell jars to reconnect to that place. You can sprinkle little bits of it into incense or candle flame when you meditate to reconnect to that place, or use it in any other spells that call for dirt. This will be a powerful addition.

Bringing Land Spirits Home

Remember that you are visiting a sacred site: taking something from an ancient temple in Greece carries a lifetime of bad luck, it is said, and I wouldn't tempt it! Leave no trace of your visit at sacred places. But you can still bring the energy of these places home with you.

If you are a crafter, I recommend bringing the ingredients or tools you need for any creative pursuits you'd like to find time for, such as watercolors, a poetry notebook, your drawing tablet, or knitting needles. Alternatively, getting tools for that craft made in or at the sacred site is an unparalleled way of inviting the energy of that place to come home with you too. While you're traveling, take time at sacred sites to work on this creative pursuit. Invite the land spirits to inspire you, and bring them into your work in a literal way too if you feel called. Sprinkle sea water from the beach you're visiting on your poetry notebook, add a pinch of dirt to the brush's water when painting, or use knot magic in thread-based crafts to literally bind the message into your work.

If you sew, knit, or crochet, begin a new project while you're traveling. Knot magic is the tying of knots toward specific goals. Knitting, crocheting, embroidery, and even yarn spinning are crafts that allow you to imbue your intentions into each stitch. Try to add some knots or stitches everywhere you visit. I recommend a small project for this, since you don't want to spend your whole trip crafting! A potholder or coaster is the best for this, as you can then use it on your altar or to otherwise remind you of your trip when you get home.

When buying souvenirs from a place, I recommend things that will invite the senses to experience that place again at home: books, spices or foods, music (make a playlist of the music you hear while on the trip), and any spiritual items customary to the culture you're visiting, such as singing bowls, statues, or ingredients for spells. Teas or dried herbs for kitchen witchery are great, as well as the free souvenirs like water from sacred springs or stones, dirt, leaves, or feathers from sacred places. Be careful of taking anything from a sacred site that could incur some serious bad energy, such as wood from a petrified forest or pottery from ancient temple grounds (seriously, it's all over the place but considered really bad luck to take!).

There and Back Again

The homeward journey can sometimes be more of a culture shock than the trip itself. When you return home, it's normal to feel a buzzing sensation, have difficulty sleeping, or sometimes worse. Feelings of depletion, exhaustion, or even depression are common after a great vacation. It's the challenge of smiling because it happened, not crying because it's over; but it's also the need to process all that went down for you.

Review your notes in your magical journal. Make a scrapbook or collage of your photos. If you created anything on the trip, place it on your altar or in the hearth of your home. Listen to the songs you heard on that trip, eat or even learn to cook the food you had, and prominently display your gifts from the land and any souvenirs you bought.

Once you've traveled more, the exhaustion and depletion start to fade and actually be replaced by a burst of energy. I often feel a flurry of productivity and inspiration upon returning home. Ride that wave. Keep it alive. This is where your sensory souvenirs will come in handy. Drink the tea, make the dishes, listen to the music, and create. Spirit-led travel is never finished even when the bags are unpacked and the laundry is put away. Remain open to new experiences, and be ready for the next opportunity.

Sometimes, it's the lessons that you're meant to learn from those particular spirits of place that make them call to you. This is an example of how land spirits are just one piece of the puzzle: you might be called to deepen your work with the deities worshiped there, the fae or elemental energies that can be met there, or the egregore itself. I find most of my spirit-led travel falls into this category of being called by the land for particular lessons. The land spirits of Malta called me there to deepen my understanding of Goddess worship in prehistoric times. The land spirits of West Virginia called me to connect to the wildness of nature in new ways. If you're being called somewhere and there's no obvious reason you can find, be open to the lessons you might receive there and continue to follow that thread.

Meditation: FOR THE NERVOUS TRAVELER

If you have trouble letting yourself enjoy things and just letting go, this is a meditation for you. This doesn't have to be for travel either. If you signed up for a book club and need the gumption to go to the meeting, or if you're starting a new exercise course and feel overwhelmed and anxious, this meditation can help too.

Preparation: In this meditation you'll be grounding and centering with your land spirits. You can do this anywhere, but if you're preparing for a trip, do this with your bags all around you, holding your passport or tickets while you do so. If you're driving to the trip, holding your car keys is another good option.

When you're ready, close your eyes. Take some deep breaths, in and out through your nose at first. Start with box breathing: inhaling for four counts, holding for four counts, then exhaling for four counts, and resting for four counts. Repeat three times, or as long as you need to to feel your heart rate come down a bit. Maintain some steady breathing, and check in with your body. Bring your shoulders down from your ears, and unclench your fists or other muscles you might be holding. Go from your neck down to your toes, taking time to unravel or release any knots or muscle tension you're holding.

Inhale as deeply as you can, for as long as you can. Feel your chest rise and your belly expand. Exhale as long and as fully as you can. Let your belly compress and your chest fall again.

Inhale slowly but deeply again, and this time focus on pulling in some of the spirit of the land. See this crisp, green light of the nature spirits around you, a warm and comforting glow. On your exhale, let that green glow stay within you, but release the dark, sludgy fears and anxieties you're having.

Again, breathe in the air of your here and now, letting yourself be filled with the familiar, warm, green, comfortable, and loving energy of your home land spirits. Exhale the inky dark worries and doubts you're feeling. As the green light fills your chest and stomach on each inhale, it starts to fill out into your legs and up into your throat, down to your feet and up to your third eye. When it reaches your crown, there's no room left inside you for any of the sludgy, viscous nervous energy. If any starts to form, trust that the loving energy of your land spirits will expel it from your head, out of your crown. Through your crown, only the grounded, stable energy of the land you call home will enter. Hold your passport or related object to your heart chakra in the center of your chest. Inhale one more soothing flow of green light, and as you exhale, feel the empty clarity in that pure breath. Open your eyes. You can now proceed on your adventure with joy and trust.

CHAPTER 10

Meeting Your True Self Through the Land Spirits

Land spirits are hard to understand at first, because of their namelessness, their locality, and their eternal, nonhuman nature of being. But when you work with them for a while, you start to notice something deeply relatable about them. Land spirits have a way of evoking your true self that is hard to explain until you too have experienced it. The crazy truth about land spirits is this: a relationship with the land is an intimacy with yourself.

In this chapter, you will find discussions and exercises that push your comfort zone. These workings are advanced, not because they require years of study, but because they require time and dedication. While all the workings in this chapter are accessible for anyone, if they feel difficult, it's okay to come back to them at a later date. I'd encourage you to do so anyway, as you grow in your relationship to land spirits, to see how you've grown and notice the differences. This is the value of your land spirits journal as well: returning to past entries will give you tangible evidence of your progress.

Connecting with land spirits is very emotional work. When you go outside and sit under a tree with your hands on her roots, sit on a rock in the middle of a creek, or stand at the peak of a mountain, you're meeting not only the land in its truest form but yourself as well.

This happens after two things are overcome.

The challenge of land spirit work is twofold. On one hand, we have to quell our ego about spirit work to really get the most out of a relationship with the land spirits. They won't give you pointed life advice, you won't get any status increase as a priest/ess/ex of the land that you might as a coven leader, and the messages or downloads you receive will likely not be words or poignant poetry but instead a simple reassuring breeze or the appearance of an animal messenger. Managing our expectations of the "wow" factor of spirit work is the first hurdle to jump.

The other expectation you'll need to release is, put simply, clarity. We often find ourselves wanting to share our spirit relationships with others, and with land spirits, it's often a case of "you had to be there" to really share the magnitude of the experiences you are having. They're the sort of magical connection with nature that children appreciate but adults laugh off. While I hope this changes as we grow as a community to embrace land spirits more intentionally, land spirit work can be a bit lonely (humanwise, anyway). It's not aesthetic on social media, it's not flashy, and it's very rarely recordable—but it is very, very powerful.

If we can manage these expectations, we can accept our relationship with the land for what it is: a moment of peace and connection, however subtle, that is purely for ourselves and our own spiritual path. The growth and depth of the work you can do with land spirits, when you accept them for what they are, is astounding. And the best way to begin to meet them is by letting your inner child lead the way.

The Inner Child as Our Guide

Embrace the land spirits by following your inner child's lead. When you go outside and look around your neighborhood, what does your inner child want to do? Does she want to dip down and smell the daffodils or pick a buttercup to see if you like butter? Is he curious what that apple tastes like straight from the orchard? Do they want to roll down that hill or hug that tree? Indulge them. Let the berry juice run down your chin. Let your nails get dirty as you lift rocks and count the different bugs on their undersides. Stop what you're doing when you walk your dog and notice a butterfly lilting on a sunflower or a squirrel chatting with a bird in a treetop. Simply taking it all in like this enables your inner child to come out and help you experience the land in an innocent way.

Innocence is to approach something with an open, kind heart and with positive expectations, if any expectations at all. What we really lose when we lose touch with our inner child is this means of interacting with the world with lightness and excitement. While it isn't always safe to live that way in a world filled with humans, nature is a place where we can reclaim our innocence. Let your inner child guide you toward that.

In the spirit of your inner child, take time outside with the land spirits to truly, really, let yourself be guided by your inner child. Remember the favorite games or imagination exercises you did when you were growing up, and then try to do them again.

If you can spare the time, visit a park where things are open and you feel comfortable to explore alone. Part of the challenge of connecting to the inner child through land spirits work is letting yourself be silly, free, and unburdened, and having others around can feel like an excuse to play small—or to let them lead. Let your inner child take the reins.

When I was a kid, I used to put birdseed on my arms and head for birds to land on me. This might be a bit much for you and understandably so; today, my knowledge of germs has me a bit horrified! But I do still love to watch the pigeons. I also loved racing the animals in my yard. We had a lot of deer in my yard growing up. If I spotted one, I would wait for it to make eye contact with me, and then when they started to run, I would run too and see who made it to the property line first (always the deer).

It may seem simple, but having unadulterated time to play is rarely taken. Turn off your phone, take off your shoes, and get dirty. Pick up a stick and draw in the dirt, watch ants carry food back to their homes, lie in the grass, or do anything you're being led to do. As long as you're not hindering your inner child, you're doing it right. These are some more ideas for things your inner child will love:

- Roll down a hill.
- Make "potions" with herbs, sticks, rocks, and other found items outdoors. Also finding the perfect stirring stick is essential!
- Flip over rocks outside in gardens and count the bugs. Try to guess before you flip it how many there will be.

- Pick up worms on a sidewalk after a rainstorm and place them back in the dirt.
- Hug trees. Smooch your houseplants.
- Climb trees. (I never could do this but if you can, be safe and enjoy!)
- Mimic birds and other animals. Bird watching is a good pairing with this activity.
- Predict how many birds will fly overhead and then count to see if you're right.
- If you live in the city, place birdseed on the ground and watch the pigeons swarm. Or try running through their favorite plaza and see how many fly with you.
- Race with animals. Make sure not to be too close; be at least 100 feet away before trying this. And be discerning about what animals you're racing! Try horses on the other side of a fence, your or a friend's dogs, or deer from a distance. It can be a great way to bond with an animal as well.

Remember to be creative—another aspect of your inner child. You don't need space or land to connect with nature, and you certainly don't have to be physically fit or even able-bodied. These are just some ideas to get you started. Your inner child will guide you the rest of the way. Record your experiences in your land spirits journal and find time to make this a regular activity.

The space land spirits grant us from the stressors of day-to-day life allows you to connect more fully with your inner child. Like a child's outlook on life, things seem manageable and just a part of the process when we trust in the support of the land. Remember too that children are resilient: they take things in stride and aren't afraid to ask questions. When we think about the importance of working with land spirits through embracing your inner child, it all comes back to our very adult shadow work as well. Through the land spirits, we can find the selves we've lost due to the world's mistreatment.

Exercise: DANCING WITH THE LAND SPIRITS

This is an exercise in vulnerability. Go outside to either your own land spirits altar or a guardian, or if that feels too public, visit a trail or national park where you can feel unobserved (by humans, at least). If it's soft underfoot, take off your shoes and do this barefoot. If it's not, no worries. The key is to have as much freedom in your movement as possible.

Directions

1. Stand with your palms out to your sides facing the ground.
2. Close your eyes and bring your energy into your palms. It should feel warm or almost numb, like an object is in your hands.
3. Keeping your eyes closed, feel the energy ball in your palms and slowly bring your palms up to the sky. Turn your wrists to lift those energy balls up to the sky, bringing your arms slowly over head.
4. Stand tall in this stretch, and gently begin moving your body how it feels good to move. Stretch, twist, lean, bend over, but keep the energy pulsing out of your palms. Throw the energy with your palms, seeing it elongate and pulse into the air around you. Feel the way it expands when you combine it between your palms, the way it sends itself upward or downward as you direct it.
5. Then, when you feel your body and your energy warmed up, begin dancing with the land. Invite the land to dance as you rotate your palms and move your hips, arms, head, shoulders, and legs. Go with the flow.
6. Notice the elementals around you and who is coming out to play. Maybe a butterfly or some bees join you. A breeze might kick up, like the air elementals inviting you to waltz. Tune in to the birds: Are they singing you an accompaniment?

7. Let ecstasy take you. If you're having trouble, try giggling! Laugh it off. This is a light, playful exercise. If big emotions come out, let yourself cry. Tears are sacred water and a gift to those we share them with. This is an offering to the land.
8. When you're ready, let the dance come to its natural end and release the energy back into the earth.

Dance is alchemy. It is an opportunity for stored energy to move through our body. It's not about how we look when we do it but how we feel. If this feels too hard, keep trying. The discipline is a key facet of land spirits work. The rewards of being able to feel energy moving up through your body like this is worth pushing through the challenges.

Silence and Contemplation

To really do the hard work of learning to listen to our emotions and the stories they come with, we need time for contemplation. We need the three *S*'s—space, solitude, and silence—in order to approach those stories.

And working with land spirits can give us all of that.

Sitting outside with no aims beyond connecting to the land gives us that space and silence, if not quite solitude. Land spirits are good listeners. They won't weigh in on specific advice, as they are beyond this world. But that is part of their charm and what makes them so companionable. If you've ever felt better after spending time with an animal, for example, you know what this feels like. Your cat didn't give you detailed advice, but they knew just how to calm you down.

Being able to tap into this space of silence and contemplation is a powerful start to the self-work that can be done with the land spirits. The following exercise is a great beginning to working with land spirits on shadow work—more on that in the next section.

Exercise: DAILY GROUNDING WITH THE LAND SPIRITS

After you get home from being out of the house, or when you begin to transition out of working for the day, go outside to your favorite tree (the same each day) and ground for 15 minutes every day for a week using this exercise. If you have a land spirits altar at this tree, all the better. This is an advanced working not because it's challenging but because it requires your attention and dedication.

Sit with your back to the tree and your palms down, touching the ground on either side of you. Close your eyes and lean back so that you feel the support of the tree on your spine. Push your hands down, if able, to feel the pulse of the earth beneath your hands. Bend your knees and put your feet, bare if possible, flat to the earth in front of you. If you have to wear gloves or shoes due to temperature, this will still work.

Feel your stressors, worries, and life's concerns flowing into the earth through your palms and the energy of the land spirits' healing flowing up in return. Lean into the support of the tree, a physical reminder of the support of the land spirits beneath and around you. Let this circuit of energy run for 15 minutes every day for a week, and record how you feel in your land spirits journal. You may decide to continue this every day or return to it when you need it.

Doing this will ground the challenges of shadow work and release them into the earth as well, while also recharging you. Feel free to repeat it as needed after intense realizations come through on your journey with getting to know your shadow. The goal of this practice is for you to feel recharged and refreshed.

Shadow Work with the Land Spirits

The inner child is a companion to our shadow. They both live within us, and with increasing experience with one or the other, we learn that they are two sides of the same coin.

Shadow work is a psychological construct, brought to witchcraft and spirituality through the work of Carl Jung in the nineteenth century. Today, as it pertains to our worldview as witches, pagans, and spiritual practitioners, shadow work is the way in which we meet our inner shadow, the parts of ourselves we shut off from the world and even ourselves because of shame, guilt, or dislike.

Through shadow work, we can learn to love our shadow self and actually embrace and accept the things we were told to be guilty about, to have shame for, or to hate about ourselves. It is a process of inner work that invites us to converse with our shadow, shine light on our perceived flaws, and reevaluate them.

Often, the roots of our shadows are something we can recognize in a new light of self-empowerment when we erase, release, or reframe our shame and guilt around it. Our shadow begins in childhood, when we're silenced for speaking too loudly or judged for our enthusiasm. This builds into beliefs about ourselves that we hold as facts, when really they're false stories. Your zest for life is a gift that should be celebrated, not quelled. Your loudness is self-expression and should be managed, not silenced. As adults, when we empower our inner child, it heals our relationship with our shadow and deepens our spiritual connection. Shadow work is a means to reclaim your power over your own story of who you are.

Shadow work is often a challenge—not only emotionally but logistically. I recommend finding a mentor, teacher, spiritual facilitator, coven, or other trusted person to witness your journey or even help you along your shadow work path. I've done shadow work alone, within a coven, and with sisterhood through online containers. All were effective, but the times I had support were much better. I also recommend working with a mental health professional in tandem with your personal shadow work, as it will provide clarity and help you process everything more fully.

Land spirits are the definition of emotional stability and grounding—truly, as eternal beings they're a-emotional. This allows us to be alone with our feelings while at the same time being calmed by the grounded presence of the land spirits enough to really feel our emotions in their presence.

Shadow work is hardest to do when we're in the thick of the struggles, pains, and fears those stories share with us. Shadow work is also difficult to do alone. It's a vulnerable process. Finding other people to help you through it can be difficult, but nature offers much healing. Land spirits are great companions. I do recommend courses, mentorship, group therapy, or one-on-one guidance if you can find the right social support to help you through your shadow work, but the land spirits are an ally not to be overlooked.

Land spirits are grounded in time out of mind. This enables them to show us our base feelings. You'll feel a primal connection to them after more and more interactions. You'll be less concerned about the pressures of the moment and more able to look at your life as if from the outside. The frustration of long commutes, the challenges of raising children, or the pipe that needs replacing in the basement will all start to fade to the background instead of creating debilitating urgency.

Exercise: JOURNAL PROMPTS FOR SHADOW WORK

Most of your experiences with your shadow will happen unbidden once you get started, but these prompts are ways to reflect and meet your shadow in an introductory way. I recommend doing this shadow work outside during your favorite weather, the kind of weather that motivates and excites you.

Though it seems counterintuitive, doing this shadow work while things are going great for yourself is the best course of action. Shadow work is an intense process in which you face the parts of yourself that you might dislike or have a negative relationship with. When you are in a good place emotionally and mentally, confronting these shadows isn't as painful and can be more productive. The days you wake up excited for life are the best days for shadow work.

Head out to your favorite tree or spot in the garden or local park with your journal and get to work. Remember: the land spirits are there to support you. Answer the following questions in your journal:

1. What are your biggest insecurities? When do you remember feeling them for the first time? Was it external forces that brought them on? How?
2. When were you most excited about something? How did the people in your life at the time react? If anyone reacted negatively, are they still in your life?
3. Who has hurt you? How? What did they tell you about yourself? How did they treat you? These are likely stories you've internalized as facts about yourself. The good news is they most definitely are not facts. People who hurt us do not have our best interests in mind when they do so, so why would we listen to them? Try this as a sentence starter: "I release opinions, criticisms, and stories told to me by ________, such as…"
4. Who are the people in your life who have lives you wouldn't mind trading with? Hopefully you like your own life most of all—but if you woke up *Freaky Friday*-ed with them, would you be okay with it? What is it about them you admire?
5. Often our shadow comes from comparing ourselves to others or trying to meet a standard we think we need to meet. But our lives are so individual that's not even possible; it's a lie told to us by society. There's no reason to feel insecure about our paths because we're the only one on them. We can't possibly judge them against another person's. Do some daydreaming about your dream life. What have you already managed and achieved? Chances are it's much more than you might have thought before beginning.

While doing shadow work, if you find yourself feeling drained or unsure of where to go, stop and pick it up another day. But before going back to your responsibilities, spend time in nature with no expectation. Try the next exercise on daily grounding. It's best to take your time with shadow work and ground fully after each session.

The Deep Longing of Hiraeth

Hiraeth is a Welsh word that means "deep longing" for something [unreachable], especially one's home.[65] Deep longing can feel like grief. The ancients understood that nostalgia was an illness: in fact, even into the nineteenth century, longing for a faraway home did lead to the deaths of soldiers.[66] Even though we know a person can die from a broken heart when grieving another person, we underestimate nostalgia for places and the impact of that on our health.

That aching in your soul almost always arises from a connection to the land spirits of a particular place. This is clear in the way we miss places we once lived or had meaningful visits to, but the ache for certain spirits of place shows itself in less direct ways as well. When we miss a person, we often are missing a time in our life, the egregore of what it felt like to be around the person. When we indulge in nostalgia for times past and the things that remind us of that time, like television shows or toys, it is that egregore of the time period we miss, the people we were at that time, and again, the spirit of the place we were in physically and emotionally.

The most complicated feeling of hiraeth you may encounter is a longing for somewhere you've never been or a time you never lived in. I have a theory that it's the land spirits themselves that we seek the connection with when our heartstrings are plucked by faraway lands. These feelings also seem to arise when we're committing to our spiritual journey, usually during the beginning stages, commonly referred to as a spiritual awakening. This is not a coincidence. Spirit-led travel holds many lessons for us, as I shared in the previous chapter.

Transmuting our grief is something the land spirits are very good at. Land spirits experience time very differently than we do, as they are eternal beings as old as the earth itself. If you've ever met a friend of a deceased loved one years after their death, you know that hearing their stories about

---

65. Chris Hopkins, "Hiraeth and Ambiguous Pastorals: Wales, England and Rural Modernities between the Wars," in *Rural Modernity in Britain*, ed. Kristin Bluemel and Michael McCluskey (Edinburgh University Press, 2018), 103.

66. Helmut Illbruck, *Nostalgia: Origins and Ends of an Unenlightened Disease* (Northwestern University Press, 2012), 32.

them and remembering them together seems to bring them to life. It can be a way to connect to them, no matter how long they've been gone. Meeting the land spirits who once knew you has the same effect. It is a way to share ourselves with others and to reconnect to our former selves.

This is why land spirits work that starts out playful, such as in the dance exercise, can lead to big emotional releases. Places, and the land spirits and guardians of them, are the keepers of what we release. They can transmute it and allow it to move through us fully as they accept our pain. The land can take it: no matter what we need to release, it cannot hurt the land. So let it flow. It's always safe to be emotionally vulnerable with land spirits.

Meditation: CONNECTING TO YOUR CHILD SELF

This meditation is best performed at a place you found great joy and power at when you were a child. If you can't get to the exact place, think about how you can get close: the nearest park, the nearest bench. Land spirits don't hold themselves to human property boundaries, so getting as close as you can will probably still be within the land spirits' area of effect.

Place yourself somewhere comfortable, with a chair or without, as you see fit. Sit or lie down in a position where you won't find your leg falling asleep or your body getting itchy or otherwise calling your attention to it over the course of 10 minutes or so.

When you're ready, close your eyes and start to breathe deeply. Let your breath guide you into calmness, breathing in and out through your nose. As you breathe, picture the clean air entering your lungs, cleansing your body. Picture this clean air tinged in a white, sanitary light, spreading throughout your body with each inhale. As it fills your body, it touches your heart, and you feel your soul reach out to this light.

On your exhale, your soul leaves your body and joins the air above your head. You can see yourself sitting in position, unmoving beneath you, as you float on a cloud of pure white light.

With each inhale, you rise higher, until you are above a cloud layer. Now on each exhale, you find yourself drifting gently beneath the cloud layer again, only this time, as the ground beneath you comes into view, you see yourself as a child, playing in the place you came here to reconnect with today. As you get closer, you see your body there, but it's the other faces that look up. They smile, nod, or greet you in their way. These are your past selves. Allow your breathing to float you gently down to sit and watch yourself play.

As you look, smiling, at your child self, they notice you. They smile back at you. Walk toward your younger self and ask them what makes them so happy about being here. Do they have a story to share with you? Allow yourself to just listen. If they hand you a stick or a stone to play with, accept it. Be the best companion for your younger self you can be.

Let them show you what they need to show you. Spend as much time here as you need to. When you're ready, hug your child self for as long as you both need that hug. Close your eyes in the vision and return yourself to your breathing.

When you're ready, open your eyes in the waking world. Write down any information you were given or describe any visions shown. Even if they don't make any sense, they might in time.

CHAPTER 11

In Sacred Relationship

Unfortunately for most of us, being outdoors and connected directly to nature isn't something we can do the majority of the time. This is a chapter filled with ways to bring the sacred wild into your life in true sacred partnership. This means letting your relationship with the land spirits affect and inspire you throughout the areas of your life, during even the most mundane activities. When you let your love of land guide your mundane life, you can deepen your relationship to the land spirits no matter how often you can get to the wilds of the world.

As I've discussed, the benefits of land spirits connection are numerous and both personal and communal. The biggest personal benefit is the grounding, stability, and ability to stay present. Many of these techniques are personal and therefore contribute to this overall need for greater grounding. In an ever-increasingly digital age, we spend less and less time outside or even connected to other humans. These practices bring the outdoors to you so that even amid digital overload, you can have a touchstone to the natural world.

The biggest communal benefit is, in a way, also stability and grounding. You are going to be a more balanced person and therefore more present for those around you. You'll also be nourished by this connection to nature and the footing in reality that will grant you. When you aren't pouring from an empty cup, you have more to offer those around you. And whenever we heal ourselves, we are healing the collective energy of our communities because of how it will affect every ripple effect we are a part of.

Being an earth intuitive means living with an empathetic relationship to the land; that means allowing your love for the earth to encompass your worldview and affect the way you make decisions. An earth intuitive learns to resist impulse buying and unnecessary purchases, recognizing that the earth is finite and capitalism is the biggest contributor to waste and pollution.

You'll begin to look for alternatives to the means of living you've become accustomed to as "normal," like using paper bags or washable containers rather than plastic baggies or using washable rags instead of paper towels. You'll become more conscious of waste in your food and recognize meal prepping as a sacred act. Farmers markets that seemed too far or inconvenient to shop at before become a reasonable expectation as you begin looking for more ways you can connect to the earth locally and therefore sustainably.

We will look at health and body as well. Our connection to our body is a connection to the land—we are an extension of land, as we're all carbon. So when we give our bodies the love and attention they deserve, nourishing them with food and moisturizing them with healthy oils and lotions, we are honoring our connection to land. We are also able to nurture our connection to nature more deeply by choosing oils and herbal infusions that align with our path and needs.

Quick connections often build long-lasting connections. When you leave the house, brush your hands over the plants you walk past or gently hug or rest against the trees on your walk to the car. If it's a fragrant plant, like lavender or rosemary, take in the scent from your hands as you continue walking. These are the ways we stay in partnership with the sacred wild: by being ready to connect and looking for opportunities.

I also want to preface this chapter by acknowledging that the overculture we face living in Western society, particularly in the United States, limits the ways we can put nature first. But what we can always control is avoiding cognitive dissonance. Cognitive dissonance is when our external actions don't align with our internal models for behavior.[67] If we say we

67. Leon Festinger, *A Theory of Cognitive Dissonance* (Stanford University Press, 1957), 3.

hold certain beliefs but act in ways that do not uphold them, we aren't living in sacred reciprocity with the land.

The goal of this chapter is to bring your awareness to the ways you can live better for the sake of the earth and thereby enhance your relationship with the land spirits by showing them you understand their needs.

In your land spirits journal, reflect on your habits and actions. Have you ever experienced guilt for your lifestyle choices? Was it valid? Consider the ways you put the earth first in your life. Write the things you're grateful to be doing and celebrate the choices you do make that are earth conscious. And if it feels like something you're motivated to do, write one thing you can do better. If you don't have any ideas yet, keep reading.

Sacred Partnership with Food

In your own garden, or in discussions with gardeners and farmers who might listen, consider the use of harsh chemicals on shrubs, lawns, gardens, and green spaces. Think more broadly. What is the alternative? Consider options like the companion planting of plants that repel pests with plants that attract them, natural insect repellants, or different ways of gardening altogether, like seasonal crop rotation. Some good alternatives to using bleach or other weed killers is white vinegar, neem oil, or baking soda. Research their effects on your biome before using even these natural alternatives. The soil, air, and fertilizers your plants eat become what you eat too.

The food we eat is an important part of our spiritual health. Ayurveda and Hindu culture teach that the food we eat is directly related to our health both physically and spiritually, but in Western spiritual practices, this understanding is often lacking.[68] Nutrition is only one part of it; you can take every supplement in the world, but if you never eat a vegetable, your body will know the difference.

Eating local produce, cheese, dairy, bread, honey, or meat is a great way to connect with your land spirits. When I was growing up in Pennsylvania's Amish country, it was said that if you eat honey from your immediate

---

68. David Frawley, *Ayurveda and the Mind: The Healing of Consciousness* (Lotus Press, 1997), 13.

vicinity (less than five miles), the pollen the bees are using is the same that you might be allergic to. Eating local honey daily is thought to mitigate your allergies to said pollen. A few studies have shown that there is scientific evidence for the effectiveness of local honey as a remedy for seasonal allergies.[69]

If you consume dairy or meat, looking for local sources isn't always easy but is doable. Consider going in on a side of beef with family and freezing it for the year's consumption, or look for chicken farmers doing small local operations of eggs or meat. You might be surprised by what's in your area that you haven't heard of. There are often farmers markets where folks travel from the surrounding counties to one local place in your area once or twice a week. See if you can get your shopping done there. Having a list is helpful to avoid overspending, as these markets can be pricier or feel inconvenient. But if you can make it work, try it for a few weeks and see if you feel the difference.

If I drive a mile up the road from my home, there's a stand in Artemis's valley with the sweetest, most glorious organic produce. This produce is inconsistent in shape, size, and availability, but 100 percent of the time, whatever I buy will taste sacred. That's the best word for it. Because it is grown in that same valley, right in front of the ancient Temple of Artemis.

The temple itself contributes greatly to the land's spiritual presence, but Artemis will be quick to remind you she was there long before the temple. A goddess of fertility, the moon, and hunting has been worshiped in that valley for at least 8,000 years, as votive offerings found in the still-functioning spring at the temple's center have shown.[70] She was not always called Artemis, but the spirit of this being has a palpable, timeless presence. She pre-dates the Greek people, as do the land spirits she surrounds herself with.

---

69. Poi Yi Aw Fahmida Islam, Hanis Hazeera Harith, Daud Ahmad Israf, Ji Wei Tan, and Chau Ling Tham, "The Potential Use of Honey as a Remedy for Allergic Diseases: A Mini Review," *Frontiers in Pharmacology* 11 (2021), doi:10.3389/fphar.2020.599080.

70. *History of Worship at the Temple Site*, Museum of the Temple of Artemis at Brauron, (Greek Ministry of Culture, 2009).

The spirits of place are strong there, as the spring is a liminal space. It is one of only three places like it in Greece where freshwater and seawater meet in thriving wetlands. The wild thyme and rosemary flower earlier there than in other parts of town, and the figs are bigger and juicier there than anywhere else. This valley is famous for its figs throughout Greece. The land is a special, spiritual place, and eating the produce from that place is worth all the inconsistencies and headache of going somewhere else for the other things I'll need. It's not uncommon for the stand to only have a few of something or only a couple of items on my shopping list. But it is an opportunity to embrace the land inside and out and be privy to the healing energy of the temple landscape each time I shop there. Even one bite of these vegetables makes it worth it.

Look at the places around you that have local produce, no matter how infrequently. If the quality is good, you'll feel it in your soul and body's health. These items can also be great offerings to your land or on your altar.

Change of Mindset

As we know, magic isn't about simply saying the right words or adding the right spell ingredients. The intention behind it is everything. Before we can tackle practices that will bring the sacred wild more intentionally into your life, we need to look at the mindset with which those practices are being done.

This is where we really start to blend the magical with the mundane. Most practitioners who have been at this for a while have come to realize that there's no need to compartmentalize your magic. The more we practice magic, the more we find ways to imbue it into our everyday life—stirring intention into the food we make, choosing the colors we wear to evoke certain expressions in ourselves and others, or shielding during difficult conversations. Checking in with the sacred wild is a lens with which to view the world, as well as a skill you'll foster until it becomes innate.

Simply put, viewing the world through the lens of the sacred wild means putting nature first. This means thinking through the choices before you in a given situation and choosing the ones that will be best for nature. Make no mistake: corporate greed is the biggest factor in pollution, waste, and harm to nature. Money is power. But that means the way we spend our money is power too. Consumer culture, especially in the United States, where online shopping is a daily occurrence for many and shopping is an activity people do for fun, not necessity, is harmful to nature. The packaging and items themselves will end up in landfills. And more than that, there are hundreds if not thousands of miles of travel, often from China on the other side of the globe, then to a warehouse, and then out directly to your own home. Pair that with the illicit production of most of these plastic items and fast fashion companies, and there's really no worse way to harm the environment than shopping online or buying cheap goods.

In Europe, especially in Greece where folks are very utilitarian and community-centered, people only buy things when something needs replacing. And not because of the latest trends, but because it truly is broken or otherwise unusable. We don't even have online shopping in most of Greece. Consumer culture in the West has gotten out of control, with people buying new decorations for every holiday, even though they probably have boxes of plenty in their basements or attics.

I've traveled extensively and lived on three continents, including in the Middle East, where consumerism, especially in the golden era of oil when I lived there in the mid-2000s, was actually worse than in modern America. And overall I've learned that the best mindset to have, in regard to putting the earth first, is a utilitarian, community-centered model: buying less, only having what you actually use or brings you joy in your life, and borrowing what else you might need. If your neighbor has a wheelbarrow, don't buy one for yourself if they're willing to share. If you have an air compressor, let your neighbor borrow it for those few times a year it's needed. The individualist culture plays into the toxicity of consumerism. Consumer advertising is playing games with that too, encouraging us all to own these things that our grandparents would have shared or even leased when needed.

This is a healthier mindset for our own mental health too. When I moved to Greece, I brought two suitcases of clothes. That's it. We got the necessary appliances—although not all the appliances we might think of as necessary in the United States. We don't have an oven (though many

Greek homes do), a clothes dryer, a dishwasher, or other things a home might have, like an ice maker or a double sink. We downsized in space too. But I found that by having less, I actually had more. More time and more energy: our only real resources. Less room and fewer belongings mean less time spent cleaning and organizing. This gave me time to write, read, connect with the land spirits—there's a very good chance that I never would've written this book if I hadn't had these changes to destress my life and give me space to consider my spiritual path and business.

My cost of living went down because Greece is a cheaper country to live in, but it also went down because I stopped shopping. I can now go weeks without spending any money; my most frequent expenditure is fresh veggies, usually under $30 each week. Living a life that puts the earth first by not overshopping, overspending, and cluttering is beneficial to you too, not just the earth. And by making these choices, your connection to the land and natural cycle of time will increase too. You won't feel guilty or removed from nature as much, opening you up to relationships with land spirits.

Although austerity and frugality are a byproduct of this mindset, it shouldn't look like suffering. In fact, you'll find you can buy better, higher-quality items. Buying less also means that when you need to replace something, like a winter coat or a new coffee maker, you might have the money to buy the fancier brand. This will last longer too, in most cases, again saving the planet from waste.

Consider how you can begin downsizing. A tip I recommend is going room by room and filling totes with items that you can't remember using in the past year or two. When you realize you need an item, go into the tote and remove it. At the end of a year, donate everything inside the tote. For things like Halloween costumes or hardware items that you might need in the future, of course there's no reason to get rid of them if you think you'll come back to them. But exercises like this help us really be able to see what's in front of us and be more aware of our belongings. In consumer culture, it can be hard to even remember all of our belongings. This practice allows us to take stock and find gratitude for what we have. Having gratitude for what we do own keeps us present, and staying present is our best bet for keeping the land focused in our practice.

At the end of the day, the harsh reality is that we aren't doing these practices to make a big difference. Sadly, even implementing every single change won't save the world or undo humanity's misdeeds. But it will improve your own relationship to the land, and that is what matters. We're always in control of our reactions: we're always in control of our magical, spiritual path. We can stay open to the opportunities that come our way to make, support, or even initiate the big changes the world needs.

Exercise: TO WHOM IT MAY CONCERN

In your land spirits journal, write a letter of concern to the corporations that are causing the destruction to the land. You can get specific or just focus on the anger and rage you feel. This letter is *not* meant to be sent, but to help you release and clear your feelings on this.

Natural Cleaning for Home and Body

Here is a quick list of natural replacements for household items I've found. These are my own lifestyle hacks I use, and you'll find my own recipes as well. I feel more connected to nature and my pagan path by making these choices. This might seem simple or too mundane, but start making the substitutions and see what happens!

Kitchen

Instead of using paper towels, use dishrags. Make your own cleaners or go to refillable stores if they're near you, instead of buying new containers with each refill. See the exercises at the end of the chapter for recipes you can use for various cleaners and removers. Look at how you can repurpose or reuse containers that are not recyclable, such as for seed germination, as food and water dishes for outdoor strays, or as containers for leftovers. Zippable plastic bags can be either eliminated completely in favor of paper bags or washable containers or washed between uses to reduce the purchase of them.

Don't fall for the marketing tricks of specialty, limited-use tools and gadgets. You don't need a special peeler just for garlic or a special tool only necessary for making one type of dish. How did your ancestors make that dish? I'm sure they have a solution using the ordinary tools you've already got!

Bathroom

Use handkerchiefs instead of napkins or tissues. Even if you're doing more laundry, this is better for the environment! Hanging your laundry, as well, if you have the time, is great for your clothes' life span and saves on energy. Using a natural product like soap nuts instead of traditional detergents is also better for the environment. Body products are often not too difficult to make yourself, even if you don't have time. You can also try buying in bulk, going to a refillable store, or choosing brands that have recyclable bottles or use recycled plastic.

Exercise: DIY CLEANING PRODUCTS AND BODY PRODUCTS

The following recipes are a perfect blend of the magical and the mundane, as they clean efficiently but can be made in a ritual or magical context to further enhance their purifying properties. All these recipes can optionally include essential oils. Choosing essential oils that invoke the qualities you need is important.

All-Purpose Cleaner

In a spray bottle, combine 2 cups of white vinegar, 1 cup of distilled water, 1 teaspoon of dish soap (pure castille soap is great), and 30 drops of essential oils if using.

Window and Glass Cleaner

Use rubbing alcohol of a strong proof and a cotton or polyester rag (cut-up t-shirt scraps work well).

Floor Cleaner

In a jar, combine 1 cup of white vinegar, 1 cup of water or an herbal tea with the properties desired, and 20 drops of essential oils, if using.

Hand Soap

Fill a foaming dispenser ¼ of the way with castile soap, add 1 teaspoon of sweet almond oil, add 1 teaspoon of glycerin, and fill the rest of the way with water. Add 25 drops of essential oil (optional).

Deodorant

Melt together ¼ cup of coconut oil, ½ cup of shea butter, 2 tablespoons of beeswax pellets, 1 tablespoon of vegetable glycerin, and 1 tablespoon of aloe vera gel together in a double boiler. Remove from heat and add ½ cup of arrowroot powder and, optionally, 1 tablespoon of baking soda.

Let cool and then add 20–40 drops of essential oil. Add more arrowroot powder if the consistency is too wet for your liking.

Body Lotion

Combine 1 cup of water and 2 cups of oil with ¼ cup of emulsifying wax in a double boiler. Add 35 drops of essential oils, or to desired smell. Tip: use oils infused with herbs from your land for an extra boost of land spirits connection.

Other Ways to Live in Partnership

There are many lessons that the sacred wild teaches that we can adopt into our lifestyles even when we aren't directly connecting to the land spirits outdoors. When we expand the perspective that all our actions affect nature, we start to live a very different life from the mainstream around us. Let's examine how that might look in a few more scenarios.

Holidays and Birthdays

Instead of giving or receiving physical gifts, instead encourage gifts of service or skill. If you are a skilled baker or cook, making someone food is a great gift. Shopping for used items to give as gifts is environmentally conscious. If you're an electrical engineer, offer to help your friend install that ceiling fan. If you do great yard work, offer to help spread mulch in the spring. If you're good at web design, help them with their website. You can also give gift certificates for these services, such as a slip of paper that says "five hours of handiwork services" if you're good at general repairs. I thank Luke on the television show *Gilmore Girls* for that idea![71] You can even get creative and create these gift certificates with extra care, decorating them with drawings, using colored paper, and hand writing them or writing personal notes on the back.

Decorations for holidays are also a big source of waste. Look for reusable items, compostable decorations, and thrifted items, and resist the urge to shop for decorations every year. If you want to make decorations every year, have at it with delightful bowls of handmade potpourri or other compostable ideas, but the constant purchasing of imported, plastic goods is tearing the planet apart.

Getting Takeaway or Delivery

When ordering food, write in the special instructions not to send cutlery or sauces. In Europe, this is a default in order to diminish waste, and you have to request them if you want them. The US hasn't caught up, at least on the East Coast where I visit, but you can request it be left out.

Grocery Shopping

Bring your own reusable net bags that can carry vegetables so you don't have to use those single-use plastic ones. In Europe, veggie bags are biodegradable, so hopefully that is close behind for the United States. Of course, as we know, bringing reusable bags to the store is important too.

---

71. *Gilmore Girls*, season 4, episode 11, "In the Clamor and the Clangor," created by Amy Sherman-Palladino (Warner Bros. Television, 2004).

I also recommend trying to buy seasonal foods. Try to take note of the origin of the produce and products you're buying. Eating out of season often means those fruits and veggies are more expensive, lower quality, and grown in a greenhouse with no access to sunlight, so these products aren't good for you at that time of year either! If you can, visit farmers markets that are locally stocked. Not all of them are—don't be afraid to ask them where their produce comes from.

Joining a co-op is great too. You're supporting local gardeners with your membership fee as well as getting fresher, more local goods. Also look into programs like Imperfect Foods or Hungry Harvest that are eliminating food waste. Often, these resources are very affordable; using Hungry Harvest in Baltimore was much cheaper than buying produce outright at the store.

Shopping

Shopping small, local, second-hand, and in person is great for community building. It gives us a chance to meet our communities and to remind ourselves that our place in them as individuals makes a difference. Your purchases from a small business will be noticed and change the lives of that business owner's family. Remember our tips from this chapter: buy less and have more of what matters, including time and energy. Opt out of getting a paper receipt whenever you can. Bring your own bags.

Lawn Care

Plant native plants, kill lantern flies or other invasive species to your area, and don't use unnatural fertilizers or sprays for weeds or growth. Avoid raking or blowing leaves anywhere you can to allow the natural cycle of decay to happen. So much wildlife is dependent on fallen leaves, especially to survive the winter. I also include in this category telling your neighbors about the damage of using bleach in the sidewalk cracks, of lawn spraying, and the like. Using pure white vinegar is better!

Travel

Traveling is by necessity bad for the environment. As I'm a spiritual traveler, this is often on my mind. I hope that my own actions help level out the fact that I fly on airplanes several times a year. Although it's controversial how much it really helps, look for airlines that are carbon neutral. I also bring my own reusable to-go coffee mug and grocery bag with me when I travel, saving me money as well as helping the environment. Takeout and restaurants can be wasteful, especially on vacation, so I am cautious when ordering to avoid waste, and I pack my own lunches often. It's also ethical to treat your accommodations like your own home, not wasting electricity or water. I opt out of getting a paper receipt when I can too. Most importantly, I've also never rented a car when I travel. Using public transport is the best way to get the flavor of a place, anyway!

Voting

I would be remiss if I didn't mention this, even though I know we all have complicated feelings about voting. No matter how silly, angry, or pointless you feel doing it, just do it. Vote for candidates who will put the environment first—or more realistically, less at the bottom of the list than the other person. Because at the end of the day, even if it means nothing, you'll know you did what you could.

Of course, these are just some considerations you might brush up against. I won't lie to you: the mental work of thinking of these things is exhausting at first. Start small and wait for the opportunities to present themselves for change, then try a new solution.

It is very overwhelming to imagine taking on all these new changes at once. Rather than seeing it as an all-or-nothing push for change, it's better to make small, lasting changes. Make it a goal to try one natural substitution from the recipes shared in the previous exercise. Take time this week or weekend to do it, and record in your land spirits journal how it feels to take sustainability into your own hands this way.

Sacred Wild Awareness

Flowers, twigs, leaves, dried fruit, cool rocks, perfect sticks, and dead insects are just some examples of nature's gifts. Often on a walk you might come across a treasure such as these that feels like a gift just for you. Bringing those indoors is a literal way to invite land spirits into your home. Place these gifts on your indoor altar, or carry them as talismans reminding you of your connection to the land.

Awareness for the sacred partnership you're cultivating is key. An advanced practice is to expand your awareness of your sacred partnership with nature through the materials you choose to use. Start considering the effects of the materials you're using for various things. Woods and stones have different qualities from each other; so too does metal versus plastic versus stone. When you need to focus the energy of a space, look into how to invite the right energies you're looking for using the right materials (or discarding the wrong ones in your space). A wooden or stone cutting board is better than plastic for this reason, as is food cooked in ceramic, copper, or steel versus a Teflon pan.

You'll find more and more ways to bring the land spirits into your life the more you try. Once you open this door to connection, let it guide you to make these choices and suggestions and to have these conversations with others. We are ambassadors for the land, the best means of representing the importance of the land's rights to other humans. When we live by example, we're helping the environment as much as possible. Let that bring peace to your mind, balance to your life, and grounding to your magical practice.

There is no ethical consumption, and being aware of that is important. At every step of the way, we need to acknowledge that and make the right choices that are in alignment with our spiritual beliefs and path. I also want to end by reminding anyone who's feeling prickly or personally attacked by any of this: there is no judgment. If you've eaten off of a paper plate because you were too tired to wash a ceramic one, don't beat yourself up about it. You're here, reading this book, and you're doing the best you can. We all fall into the easy, capitalism-suggested choices at times. It's all about making the necessary steps and adjustments, little by little, and as we can manage mentally, physically, and financially.

Meditation: INVITING THE LAND SPIRITS INDOORS

This is a meditation best performed when you're in need of some natural connection. If you're dragging through your day, feeling low on energy and positivity, this is a quick connection to the land you can do subtly. At the least, even if you're not adept at visualizing, this meditation should remind you of the connection of the time of year and help you stay present in the long run.

Bring your attention to your breathing, but without stressing yourself out about breathing in too deeply if there aren't pleasant smells where you are! Keeping your breath steady and not too shallow, focusing on inhaling and exhaling through your nose, and walk yourself outdoors in your mind's eye. You can do this with your eyes open and staring unfocused at a stationary, plain object in front of you, like a cubicle wall, your desk, or even the floor.

Now, in your mind's eye, you are outside of the building you're currently in. What is the weather outside? The temperature? Dry or damp? How does the air feel on your bare skin? What does the sky look like? What sounds, of nature or otherwise, can you hear outside? Now imagine you're lifting up into the sky and the office is getting smaller and smaller beneath you. What's the nearest nature to you? Can you see the sea or a patch of forest? Is there a river, lake, or pond nearby? Are there birds flying through the sky around you as you hover within the clouds?

Now drift yourself back down to earth. As you land, feel the ground beneath your feet. Let your earthly body settle your feet to the ground solidly too, but imagine its grass or soil beneath you instead of the indoor floor. Feel the energy of those nearby natural sites in the earth beneath you. Let it travel to you, as slowly or as quickly as it may. Focus on the settling of it under your feet, as if you can feel the thousands of roots and tunnels in the soil beneath you. A slightly warm sensation tingles the bottom of your feet, a golden light surrounding the ground you're standing on.

As it continues to warm your feet and glow around you, invite the spirit of the land to join the space. In your head, ask the land spirits to stand with you and charge the energy beneath your feet with their powers of calm, ageless presence. Ask that they allow this energy to accompany you inside.

Let that warm, golden energy of nature and the spirits of the land flow upward into your body through the soles (souls?) of your feet.

Like a flower's stem drinking water from the ground, you're filling yourself up with the grounded, stable energy of the land spirits. Allow the golden light to fill you up, charging your kundalini and your own energy centers as it rises to your crown. Let it flow out of your crown and fill the space your earthly body inhabits indoors. Let it cleanse and purify the stagnant energy of the room you're in.

When you're ready, open your eyes. The room should feel clearer and brighter.

Conclusion

As I write these final words, the sacred wild is speaking to me at my window. Night has fallen, and the wind is whistling in long, high tones. Here in Greece, I'm by the sea, where wind speeds have always been higher than further inland. But each passing year, they reach record speeds. The neighborhood cats I care for are hunkered down in their cat houses on the patio, and the *pevka* pine trees are whipping in the wind. And I know, deep in my spiritual core, that it is a call to action.

Reflecting on the state of the world breeds powerful emotions that we can use to spur us on toward action. That is the magic the land needs from us. The rage that nature manifests in whipping winds, mudslides, forest fires, and hailstorms can be translated into action. Emotions are energy, a very powerful force of energy. Magic is energy manipulation: using our will to direct energy where we want. Land spirits provide a fantastic grounding for emotional direction, making them allies for protection, shadow work, and higher-self exploration. But they also remind us that in our connection to all things, when we have control over our energy, we can do anything we want to in this world.

As you go forth on your journey of connection with the land, remember that the land is calling to you for a reason. The land is suffering at the hands of human action—but so are humans. For this reason, we must stand together with the land, now more than ever. We can only weather the storms to come, in our personal lives and globally, if we meet them head on with nature at our side. Inviting the sacred wild is about listening to the land and letting the land listen to you—and the next step is speaking up, together.

As you embrace the sacred wild, be open to how you can be the voice for nature. Nature can certainly speak for itself too, as we've seen in climate calamities, and it's up to us, the witches, pagans, and spiritual folks who live at the crossroads, to be the conduit for their magic—and through this, strengthen our own.

I've enjoyed a quiet union with the land spirits all my life, but when that fox crossed my path, I knew it was time to amplify their voices. Many of these exercises began as channeled workings of my own. While I wrote the book itself, the land guided my hand at every turn.

I hope it will do the same for you.

Glossary

Egregore: The energy of a place that includes all the layers of spirits that might inhabit it. It is the most present energy in a given place. In places with a lot of humans, it's often a very thick energetic layer. You will feel this first and foremost, so when seeking to work with land spirits, you will need to reach beneath this.

Elders: Extremely old formations and natural places in the landscape, such as lakes, deserts, rivers, forests, and so on that are elders of land in their age and presence in that place. These are the places land spirits are most acutely felt.

Elementals: Transient spirits that are expressions of their given element. For example, the water elementals can be spirits found in a particular river, the river being an elder spirit that those elementals coexist with.

Emissaries: Any animal living on that land that chooses to connect or communicate with you. These are often creatures that communicate to us on behalf of the land spirits, and they serve as a front line to the land spirits' energy.

Guardians: The individual trees, small creeks, little crevasses, or boulders that are connected to larger elders of land. These are gatekeepers to meeting and connecting with the land spirits.

Land Spirits: The spirit of the land found only at that particular location. Land spirits' areas of effect vary: they can spread across a whole neighborhood or be concentrated in a particular grove of trees. There can be more than one land spirit present in a particular place, but there is usually one presiding land spirit that can be accessed through elders or guardians, and emissaries or vassals can be how they communicate with you, as well as through elementals and weather spirits.

Plant Spirits: Every plant you encounter has a twofold spirit that is collectively referred to as "the spirit of the plant" or a "plant spirit." This is the spirit of a particular plant species, but it also refers to the spirit of the individual plant you will meet. Just like all humans have human qualities in common, so too do all rosemary plants share the plant spirit of Rosemary. But each individual rosemary plant has an individual spirit to it as well. This combined sense of self is the plant spirit you can engage with. You can meet the egregore of Rosemary without the physical plant in front of you as well.

Spirits of Place: All spirits you'll find in a given place are spirits of place: the land spirits, the weather spirits, the wind spirits, the plant spirits … They are all spirits of a given place.

Vassals: Groups of emissary animals that hold dominion in this land. For example, your land might be home to a murder of crows that feel like the leading emissaries of your land—think of vassals as the most commonly found animals or insects of your space.

Weather Spirits: Transient spirits that travel with particular weather (e.g., wind spirits, spirits of the hurricane, etc.).

Wind Spirits: Spirits of air. They are often very communicative, and the land spirits like to let you know they're listening by collaborating with the wind to blow when you give an offering or ask for a sign. They almost act like emissaries in this way.

Annotated Recommended Reading List

Ballard, Byron H. *Small Magics: Practical Secrets from an Appalachian Village Witch*. Llewellyn Publications, 2023.

This is a great resource on working with the land in simple ways. Her book *Roots, Branches, and Spirits* is also fantastic, but this one was actually my favorite of all her works.

Bedell, Charity L. *Divine Dirt: A Wealth of Spells for Incorporating Types of Dirt in Your Practice*. Llewellyn Publications, 2024.

This book offers as collection of magic and guidance for working with dirt.

Billington, Penny. *Nine Ways to Charm a Dryad: A Magical Adventure to Connect with the Spirit of Trees*. Llewellyn Publications, 2022.

An OBOD Druid author, the editor of *Touchstone*, OBOD's magazine, she is one of my favorite teachers of tree magic specifically.

Burris, Deborah. *Weather Magic: Witchery, Science, Lore*. Llewellyn Publications, 2024.

An invaluable source for the weather magic chapter of this book, this is the authoritative book on weather magic for sure. Everything from rain to hurricanes and tornadoes is covered in depth, as well as fun explorations on traditional sayings about weather and if they are true or false.

Crombie, R. Ogilvie. *Encounters with Nature Spirits: Co-creating with the Elemental Kingdom*. Findhorn Press, 2018.

More of a narrative of the author's personal experience, this is a great look at what nature spirit work can look like from another perspective.

Forest, Danu. *Nature Spirits: Wyrd Lore and Wild Fey Magic*. Wooden Books, 2008.

This is a bit more of an artistic book of drawings than a practical guide for practicing witches or pagans, but it is certainly inspiring.

Hughes, Kristoffer. *The Book of Druidry: A Complete Introduction to the Magic & Wisdom of the Celtic Mysteries*. Llewellyn Publications, 2023.

Hughes is chief of the Anglesey Druid Order, a Mount Haemus Scholar, and a member of the Order of Bards, Ovates, and Druids. This book is also a journal that guides you through Druidic connection to land, sea, and sky.

Hutton, Ronald. "Modern Druidry and Earth Mysteries." *Time & Mind: The Journal of Archaeology, Consciousness and Culture* 2, no. 3 (2009): 313–31. doi:10.2752/175169609X12464529903137.

A solid academic article (like everything Hutton writes) that dives into the connections of earth and spiritual mystery from a modern Druidic perspective.

Hunter, Devin. *Houseplant HortOCCULTure: Green Magic for Indoor Spaces*. Llewellyn Publications, 2022.

A comprehensive guide to raising plants indoors for greater connection to nature.

Johnson, Elizabeth A. *Women, Earth, and Creator Spirit*. Paulist Press, 1993.

An essay on ecofeminism.

Kimmerer, Robin Wall. *Braiding Sweetgrass: Indigenous Wisdom, Scientific Knowledge, and the Teachings of Plants*. Milkweed Editions, 2013.

This is *the* book on the intersection of ecology (the science) with ecocentrism (the practice). As an Indigenous American woman and a doctor and professor of ecology, Kimmerer's perspectives on sacred reciprocity come from the full spectrum of possible angles. The biggest takeaway from her book is that we are not parasites; we are meant to be on Earth. If you feel guilty for existing as a human, and that is eating away at you and blocking you from practicing, this is the book to change your life.

Kirner, Kimberly. *American Druidry: Crafting the Wild Soul.* Bloomsbury, 2024.

An academic text, this is the best book on what Druidry looks like in America.

Kynes, Sandra. *Tree Magic: Connecting with the Spirit & Wisdom of Trees.* Llewellyn Publications, 2021.

The correspondences guru, Kynes explores the different types of trees you can connect to for which magical purposes.

Larson, Jennifer. *Greek Nymphs: Myth, Cult, Lore.* Oxford University Press, 2001.

An academic text, this is the only book exclusively on nature spirits of Greece. It is out of print, but PDFs are available through JSTOR and other academic databases.

Lecouteux, Claude. *Demons and Spirits of the Land: Ancestral Lore and Practices.* Translated by Jon E. Graham. Inner Traditions, 2015.

This book includes rituals from a variety of cultural contexts to connect with land.

Matthews, Caitlín, and John Matthews. *Walkers Between the Worlds: The Western Mysteries from Shaman to Magus.* Inner Traditions, 2003.

The authors are two of my favorite earth-based spiritual writers in the world. They have a distinct shamanic approach to nature and the lessons she has for us, based in Celtic and British folklore and experience.

McCoy, Edain. *A Witch's Guide to Faery Folk: How to Work with the Elemental World.* Llewellyn Publications, 1994.

For those most interested in the fae from a Celtic perspective.

McKay, Dodie Graham. *Earth Magic*. Llewellyn Publications, 2021.
Part of the Elements of Witchcraft series, this book is more than an introduction to earth as an element. It is a conversation, featuring contributors from many different backgrounds, including Indigenous North American tribes. The introduction also explains the history of witchcraft as an earth-based spiritual practice, which is helpful and concise.

Myers, Brendan. *The Earth, the Gods, and the Pagan Soul: A History of Pagan Philosophy from the Iron Age to the 21st Century.* Moon Books, 2013.
By an OBOD Druid, this is a deep dive into the philosophy behind earth-based spirituality, or paganism.

Pearson, Nicholas. *Flower Essences from the Witch's Garden: Plant Spirits in Magickal Herbalism*. Destiny Books, 2022.
An inspiration for anyone looking deeper into flower essences and the many ways to make and use them.

Pogačnik, Marko. *Nature Spirits & Elemental Beings: Working with the Intelligence in Nature.* Findhorn Press, 1997.
This book includes firsthand accounts of working with land work as healing—particularly in healing the earth herself—through meditation.

Raven, Susan. *Nature Spirits: The Remembrance*. Clairview, 2012.
This book is a guide to connecting consciously to the earth.

Starhawk. *Spiral Dance: A Rebirth of the Ancient Religion of the Great Goddess.* 20th anniv. ed. HarperSanFrancisco, 2011.
This is the foundational text for the eclectic Faery Tradition and explains the interconnectedness of energy as a spiral. She is one of the great elders of the twentieth century.

Sullivan, Danny. *Ley Lines: The Greatest Landscape Mystery*. Green Magic, 2004.
Discussing ley lines and their connection to sacred places.

Tolkien, J. R. R. *The Lord of the Rings.* HarperCollins, 2004.
An affectual handbook on animism—never underestimate the power of fiction to teach us. This is the book that inspired my connection to nature as a child and is a foundational text for bibliomancy for me. If it doesn't resonate with you, don't force it; but if *LotR* calls to you as it has me, reading it through the lens of animism is enlightening in memorable ways. Our ancestors used myth to remember and learn, and so too can we.

Wohlleben, Peter. *The Hidden Life of Trees: What They Feel, How They Communicate—Discoveries from a Secret World.* Translated by Jane Billinghurst. Greystone Books, 2016.
The science and ecological background to how trees live and guide the ecosystems they are a part of. There is so much power in this knowledge.

Bibliography

Aesop. *Aesop's Fables*. Guizhou Renming Publisher, 2009.

Anonymous. *The Encyclopedia of Occult Sciences*. Robert M. McBride & Co., 1939.

Bahram, Mohammad, and Tarquin Netherway. "Fungi as Mediators Linking Organisms and Ecosystems." *FEMS Microbiology Reviews* 46, no. 2 (2022): fuab058. doi:10.1093/femsre/fuab058.

Berg, T. M., W. E. Edmunds, A. R. Geyer, and other compilers. *Geologic Map of Pennsylvania.* 2nd ed. Map 1. Pennsylvania Geologic Survey, 1980. 1:250,000 scale.

Boyd, James W., and Ron G. Williams. "Japanese Shintō: An Interpretation of a Priestly Perspective." *Philosophy East and West* 55, no. 1 (2005): 33–63. http://www.jstor.org/stable/4487935.

Bradbury, Scott. "Constantine and the Problem of Anti-Pagan Legislation in the Fourth Century." *Classical Philology* 89, no. 2 (1994): 120–39. https://doi.org/10.1086/367402.

Burris, Deborah. *Weather Magic: Witchery, Science, Lore.* Llewellyn Publications, 2024.

Clive, Ruggles. *Ancient Astronomy: An Encyclopedia of Cosmologies and Myth*. ABC-CLIO, 2005.

Crowley, Aleister. *The Book of the Goetia of Solomon the King*. Society for the Propagation of Religious Truth, 1904.

Cunningham, Scott. *Earth Power: Techniques of Natural Magic*. Llewellyn Publications, 1983.

Debus, Allen G. "Paracelsus and the Medical Revolution of the Renaissance: A 500th Anniversary Celebration." *Paracelsus, Five Hundred Years: Three American Exhibits*. The Friends of the National Library of Medicine, 1993. Exhibition brochure.

Farrar, Janet, and Stewart Farrar. *The Witches' Way: Principles, Rituals and Beliefs of Modern Witchcraft*. Phoenix Publishing, 1984.

Festinger, Leon. *A Theory of Cognitive Dissonance*. Stanford University Press, 1957.

Frawley, David. *Ayurveda and the Mind: The Healing of Consciousness*. Lotus Press, 1997.

Gilmore Girls. Season 4, episode 11, "In the Clamor and the Clangor." Created by Amy Sherman-Palladino. Warner Bros. Television, 2004.

Graves, Charles, and C. Limerick. "The Ogham Alphabet." *Hermathena* 2, no. 4 (1876): 443–72. https://www.jstor.org/stable/23036451.

Griffith, Ralph T. H., trans. *The Hymns of the Rigveda*. Motilal Banarsidass, 1973.

Helbich, Marco. "Mental Health and Environmental Exposures: An Editorial." *International Journal of Environmental Research and Public Health* 15, no. 10 (2018): 2207. doi:10.3390/ijerph15102207.

Heritage Malta. Exhibition materials and curator interview with the author. Hal Saflieni Hypogeum. Malta, 2023.

History of Worship at the Temple Site. Museum of the Temple of Artemis at Brauron. Greek Ministry of Culture, 2009.

Hoggard, Brian. "Protective Marks Lecture with Brian Hoggard." Churches Conservation Trust. May 27, 2020. YouTube, 33:21. https://www.youtube.com/watch?v=kHTG_xxpQzI.

Homer. *The Homeric Hymns*. Translated by J. Edgar. Legare Street Press, 2023.

Hopkins, Chris. "*Hiraeth* and Ambiguous Pastorals: Wales, England and Rural Modernities between the Wars." In *Rural Modernity in Britain*. Edited by Kristin Bluemel and Michael McCluskey. Edinburgh University Press, 2018.

Illbruck, Helmut. *Nostalgia: Origins and Ends of an Unenlightened Disease.* Northwestern University Press, 2012.

Ingram, John Henry. *Flora Symbolica; or, the Language and Sentiment of Flowers*. London: Frederick Warne and Co, 1870.

Ivakhiv, Adrian J. *Claiming Sacred Ground: Pilgrims and Politics at Glastonbury and Sedona*. Indiana University Press, 2001.

Jamison, Stephanie W., and Joel P. Brereton, trans. *The Rigveda: The Earliest Religious Poetry of India*. 3 vols. Oxford University Press, 2014.

Jones, Prudence. "A Goddess Arrives: Nineteenth Century Sources of the New Age Triple Moon Goddess." *Culture and Cosmos* 9, no. 1 (2005): 47–71. doi:10.46472/cc.0109.0205.

Kinealy, Christine. *The Great Irish Famine: Impact, Ideology, and Rebellion.* Palgrave, 2002.

Łaszkiewicz, Weronika. "Into the Wild Woods: On the Significance of Trees and Forests in Fantasy Fiction." *Mythlore* 36, no. 1 (2017): 39–58. https://www.jstor.org/stable/26809256.

Larson, Jennifer. *Greek Nymphs: Myth, Cult, Lore*. Oxford University Press, 2001.

Lucian of Samosata. *Dialogues of the Gods*. In *The Works of Lucian of Samosata.* Vol 1. Translated by H. W. Fowler and F. G. Fowler. Clarendon Press, 1905. Electronic reproduction by Sacred Texts Archive. https://sacred-texts.com/cla/luc/wl1/wl113.htm.

MacDonald, George. *At the Back of the North Wind.* London: Strahan & Co., 1871.

McKay, Dodie Graham. *Earth Magic*. Llewellyn Publications, 2021.

Morgan, Gerald. "The Significance of the Pentangle Symbolism in 'Sir Gawain and the Green Knight.'" *The Modern Language Review* 74, no. 4 (1979): 769–90. doi:10.2307/3728227.

Otto, Carolyn. *Celebrate Kwanzaa: With Candles, Community, and the Fruits of the Harvest*. National Geographic, 2017.

Paracelsus. *Four Treatises of Theophrastus von Hohenheim, Called Paracelsus*. Vol. 1. Edited by C. Lilian Temkin, George Rosen, Gregory Zilboorg, and Henry E. Sigerist. Johns Hopkins Press, 1941.

Pausanias. *Pausanias's Description of Greece.* Translated and edited by J. G. Frazer. 6 vols. Cambridge University Press, 2012.

Pearson, Nicholas. *Flower Essences from the Witch's Garden: Plant Spirits in Magickal Herbalism*. Destiny Books, 2022.

Pinto, Eliseo Mauas. *Celtic Tree Wisdom and Magick.* Pubished by the author, 2013.

Raedisch, Linda. *The Old Magic of Christmas: Yuletide Traditions for the Darkest Days of the Year.* Llewellyn Publications, 2013.

"Rain Dance." *International Feminist Journal of Politics* 9, no. 4 (2007): 558–59. doi:10.1080/14616740701608307.

Roman, Luke, and Monica Roman. *Encyclopedia of Greek and Roman Mythology*. Facts On File, 2010.

Smith, Eric C. "The History of the Catacombs." In *Foucault's Heterotopia in Christian Catacombs*. Palgrave Macmillan, 2014.

Stavish, Mark. *Egregores: The Occult Entities That Watch Over Human Destiny*. Inner Traditions, 2018.

Till, Rupert. "An Archaeo Acoustic Study of the Ħal Saflieni Hypogeum on Malta." *Antiquity* 91, no. 355 (2017): 74–89. doi:/10.15184/aqy.2016.258.

Tolkien, J. R. R. *The Lord of the Rings*. HarperCollins, 2004.

Virgil. *The Aeneid: Books I–VI.* Edited by T. E. Page. London: Macmillan, 1894.

Whitehead, P. G., E. Barbour, M. N. Futter, S. Sarkar, H. Rodda, J. Caesar, et al. "Impacts of Climate Change and Socio-Economic Scenarios on Flow and Water Quality of the Ganges, Brahmaputra and Meghna (GBM) River Systems." *Environmental Science: Processes & Impacts* 17, no. 6 (2015): 1057–69. doi:10.1039/C4EM00619D.

Wilde, Jane. *Ancient Legends, Mystic Charms, and Superstitions of Ireland.* Boston: Ticknor and Company, 1888.

Witchwood, Leandra, and Elyse Welles, hosts. *The Magick Kitchen Podcast*. Season 7, episode 9, "Community Mindsets Rooted in Simple, 'Small' Magic: The Lessons of Appalachian Folk Practice with Byron Ballard." April 8, 2024. https://www.themagickkitchen.com/podcast/.

Wright, Laura. *Sunnyside: A Sociolinguistic History of British House Names*. Oxford University Press, 2020.

Yong, Poi Yi Aw, Fahmida Islam, Hanis Hazeera Harith, Daud Ahmad Israf, Ji Wei Tan, and Chau Ling Tham. "The Potential Use of Honey as a Remedy for Allergic Diseases: A Mini Review." *Frontiers in Pharmacology* 11 (2021). doi:10.3389/fphar.2020.599080.

To Write to the Author

If you wish to contact the author or would like more information about this book, please write to the author in care of Llewellyn Worldwide Ltd. and we will forward your request. Both the author and the publisher appreciate hearing from you and learning of your enjoyment of this book and how it has helped you. Llewellyn Worldwide Ltd. cannot guarantee that every letter written to the author can be answered, but all will be forwarded. Please write to:

Elyse Welles
℅ Llewellyn Worldwide
2143 Wooddale Drive
Woodbury, MN 55125-2989

Please enclose a self-addressed stamped envelope for reply, or $1.00 to cover costs. If outside the U.S.A., enclose an international postal reply coupon.

Many of Llewellyn's authors have websites with additional information and resources. For more information, please visit our website at http://www.llewellyn.com.

Notes

Notes